MW00414767

Core Creativity

DISCLAIMER

This book does not prescribe treatment for any specific psychological, medical, or physical condition. The information contained herein is provided as public service. It is included for informational and educational purposes only and should not be construed as personal medical advice and should not be used for diagnosing or treating a medical or emotional problem or condition. Always seek professional advice with any questions you may have regarding a particular medical or psychological issue. Reliance on any information provided in this book is solely at your own risk. The publisher and author assume no responsibility for your actions. Nothing in this book is designed to cure specific physical or psychological disorders or diseases.

The visualizations and meditations in this book can complement treatments you are receiving from medical and psychological health care providers. Check with your health care providers about the appropriateness of using these practices in tandem with the treatment you are receiving.

Stories of individuals in this book have had details altered to protect confidentiality.

Core Creativity

The Mindful Way to Unlock Your Creative Self

Ronald Alexander, PhD

ROWMAN & LITTLEFIELD
Lanham • Boulder • New York • London

Published by Rowman & Littlefield
An imprint of The Rowman & Littlefield Publishing Group, Inc.
4501 Forbes Boulevard, Suite 200, Lanham, Maryland 20706
www.rowman.com

86-90 Paul Street, London EC2A 4NE

A meditation similar to the Body Observation Meditation, with similar variations, called Sweeping Body Meditation, appeared in Ronald Alexander, PhD, *Wise Mind Open Mind: Finding Purpose and Meaning in Times of Crisis, Loss, and Change*, Oakland, CA: New Harbinger Publications, 2008, pages 66–67.

The paragraph describing open mind that appears at the beginning of chapter 5 is from *Wise Mind, Open Mind* by Ronald A. Alexander, PhD, published in 2008 by New Harbinger Publications, Inc.

British Library Cataloguing in Publication Information Available

Library of Congress Cataloging-in-Publication Data

Names: Alexander, Ronald A., author.
Title: Core creativity for everyone : the mindful way to unlocking your creative self / Ronald Alexander, PhD.
Description: Lanham : Rowman & Littlefield Publishing, [2022] | Includes bibliographical references and index. | Summary: "Offers ways to upgrade creativity while practicing mindfulness so that anyone can achieve breakthroughs in any area of their life. Looking to upgrade your creative abilities? Core Creativity offers ways to go beyond the limitations of ordinary creativity to access the core creativity that comes from the very center of your being: the depths of your unconscious. Ronald Alexander has decades of experience working with core creatives—artists who regularly draw on deep creativity and have learned what to do when the well seems to have run dry. Using mindfulness practice, meditation and visualizations, and habits and mindsets of highly creative people, anyone can experience the flow of ideas as if from an infinitely abundant source. Core Creativity employs stories of ordinary but highly creative people alongside the latest research that helps people get unstuck. Too often, the mind's Wi-Fi signal is too weak for the really big ideas to load, but Core Creativity offers readers help with establishing a mindfulness practice; exercises for enhancing creativity and fostering better decision-making; key insights from personal interviews with highly creative artists including music producer Val Garay, director Amy Ziering, and actor Denis Quaid; and guidance for reclaiming your creative self so you can achieve profound transformation. Core creativity allows you to come up with ideas that are both fresh and original and experience such a deep state of creative flow that it might feel as if you only played a minor role in the process of creativity. For anyone seeking to enhance their creative abilities and achieve their goals, Core Creativity presents the possibility of genuine breakthroughs"—Provided by publisher.
Identifiers: LCCN 2021054071 (print) | LCCN 2021054072 (ebook) | ISBN 9781538149560 (cloth) | ISBN 9781538149577 (epub)
Subjects: LCSH: Creative ability. | Creative thinking.
Classification: LCC BF408 .A456 2022 (print) | LCC BF408 (ebook) | DDC 153.3/5—dc23/eng/20211122
LC record available at https://lccn.loc.gov/2021054071
LC ebook record available at https://lccn.loc.gov/2021054072

Contents

Acknowledgments

I want to thank my first teachers of Zen meditation and Tai Chi Chuan, Teresina Havens, Ph.D., Edward Espé Brown, and Daniel Wang, Vipassana meditation Jack Kornfield, Ph.D; and Joseph Goldstein. My earliest and ongoing teachers of Tibetan Buddhism, colleague and lifelong friend Daniel P Brown, Ph.D., Tsoknyi Rinpoche and Lama Tharchin Rinpoche. Baba Hari Dass, Shiva Rea and Derek Ireland my Ashtanga yoga teachers and my lifelong mentor and transpersonal clinical guide Ram Dass, Ph.D. who encouraged me to aspire to the highest values and to become somebody first but then to let go and surrender into Nobody.

A heartfelt thank you to Suzanne Staszak my publisher at Rowman & Littlefield for purchasing this book.

I also want to acknowledge the extraordinary creatives who blessed me with their time, energy, and enormous creative insights through hours of interviews distilled down to bite size wisdom for this book: Cody Fern, Val Garay, Ronnie Landfield, Jodi Long, Dennis Quaid, Jonathan Scales, David Seltzer, Yaro Starak, and Amy Ziering. I am in awe and deeply appreciative of their talents and creative wisdom.

To my many friends, colleagues, and members of both my councils of support, creativity pods and teachers throughout the years, whose friendship and support means the world to me: Alan Arkles; Joel Behr (for his creative and legal expertise); Jim Blechman, MD; Karen Bohan, MA; Katie Brauer; Tara Brach PhD; Ken Dychtwald PhD; Jenny Boyd-Levitt, PhD; Jim Clancy, MA; Debra Clydesdale, LAc; Eleanor Criswell, PhD; Ben Decker; Vera Dunn, PhD; Corey Folsom; James

Fadiman, PhD (for his insights and exactness on the microdosing section); Pamela Fields, PhD, (for decades of creative reflections); Rob and Tracy Donnell; Diane Poole Heller, PhD; Stephen Gilligan, PhD; Robert Guerette, MD; Anita Jung, MS; Loch Kelly, LCSW; Paige Brewster-Kelly, LCSW; Ursula Klich PhD; Carl Greer PhD; Elisha Goldstein PhD; Jack Kornfield PhD; Trudy Goodman-Kornfield PhD; Stanley Krippner, PhD; Carl Kugel, MA; Sebastian Lampe MS; Ellen Langer, PhD; Peter A Levine, PhD; Teri Lindeman, MA; Jodi Long (so many wonderful creative connections); Bill O'Hanlon; Ora Nadrich MS; Judith Orloff, MD (expansive co-creative); Nicola Lynch-Morrin; Erving Polster, PhD; Emma Farr Rawlings, PhD (her steadfast and unyielding focus with WMOM); Harvey Rudarian; Shiva Rea, MA; Robert Resnick, PhD; Lorin Roche, PhD; Ronald Siegel Psy.D; Sharon Salzberg; Ashley Turner, MA; Alberto Villoldo, PhD; Bruce Vinokour at CAA; Sarah Wadsworth; Radhule Weininger, PhD; and Jeffery Zeig, PhD.

And to all those unnamed throughout my vast worldly network I honor and bow to so many important relationships, both living and now passed onto the other side.

To my right-hand and longtime professional assistant, Rhonda Bryant who multi-faceted expertise and assistance are forever deeply appreciated and valued beyond words. To my team of assistants Kelly Hampton who sent out the book proposal and made the connection with Rowman & Littlefield and Debra Yates, for years of devoted service deep appreciation.

To my navigator, co-creative collaborator, the rhythm guitar to my lead, the multitalented Nancy Peske whose professional skill sets bring a polish and refinement to my images, ideas, and words, I am so grateful to you for your excellent counsel, guidance, and support.

Chapter One

The Deepest Creativity
Comes from Your Core

Not long ago, I was standing in the recording studio at the home of a highly talented and successful guitarist who also sings and writes songs. He knows me through friends and family, and we had spent the better part of an evening talking about his various projects. While he is known best for his music, he has been involved in other arts. I've always been impressed by his internal drive to keep expressing himself in new ways and collaborating with new people.

The two of us had been talking about one of the key elements to his productivity: regular practice sessions with fellow musicians and songwriters. He explained that he had a long-established habit of carving out a workday that involved playing songs, improvising, talking about music and art, and letting the creative juices flow. A rotation of musicians—old friends and new—come through his studio at his home. These fellow musicians offer him new ideas, riff off the ones that he comes up with, and keep the flow going.

I said to him, "You know, I've always found it curious that people who are out of touch with their creativity assume that creative people have no discipline—that they just distract themselves day after day until the muse strikes. I've never found that to be true. Creative artists are among the most disciplined people I know."

The musician nodded his assent and reached out with his fingers, sliding them gently across the strings of one of his guitars, which was resting on a stand. "But sometimes . . . the guitar just speaks to me."

I understood what he was saying: his creativity comes from a deeper place than simply trying to "figure out" what would sound right for a particular song. His movement back and forth among all the stages of creativity—waiting for inspiration without procrastinating, playing and practicing in a disciplined way, taking in new stimulation—is, for him, as natural as breathing. He's in touch with his core creativity, someone who knows how to get to the deepest levels of innovative ability and can rely on that strength to sustain a livelihood in a field that demands creativity.

You might not even think of yourself as being creative, but there is much you can learn from highly creative people and their processes that will turn up the volume on your own creativity. You might be hoping to become more creative and experience a breakthrough so that you can bring about much-desired personal transformation or because you have experienced a significant loss (or are about to do so) that's forcing change upon you. Billions of people around the world were jolted out of the belief that life would go on as always when the COVID-19 pandemic began. Many became very anxious or depressed, not knowing how to adjust to the new reality.

You might also be hoping to become more creative to sustain and build your career at a time of tremendous change due to pandemics, globalization, climate change, technological advances, and other forces that will result in changes for you and others. We're not even sure what types of jobs will be available in the future—and which won't be. In the 1980s, I began working with many record company executives whose identities were deeply enmeshed in their careers and who saw the writing on the wall. A new technological innovation, an online service called Napster that allowed people to share musical recordings with others for free, came online in the early 1990s and altered the music business landscape overnight. Recognizing that the number of record labels would be dramatically reduced, these executives felt that if they hadn't already lost their jobs, they would soon. With no idea what their next chapter would be, they sought a breakthrough in their thinking that would clear the fog. They knew there was no way to stop the huge wave headed their way.

Given the pace of radical change all over the world, schools ought to be training students to tap into and use their creativity. A recent LinkedIn analysis of their data showed that the number one soft skill employers are looking for is creativity.[1] A recent survey of employers by the American Management Association showed that 75 percent felt that creativity was a key skill employees needed.[2] And a 2015 *Forbes* magazine article, "The Rise of Creativity as a Key Quality in Modern Leadership," reported that "[t]he last two decades have seen nearly all businesses embrace innovation and creativity as central missions, at least at a high level, with leaders expected to serve as imaginative guides."[3] Are these leaders up to the task?

One thing is for certain: the world needs creativity right now. As author, ethnobotanist, and philosopher Terence McKenna has said, "You are an explorer, and you represent our species, and the greatest good you can do is to bring back a new idea—because our world is in danger by the absence of good ideas. Our world is in crisis because of the absence of consciousness. And so to whatever degree any one of us can bring back a small piece of the picture and contribute it to the building of the new paradigm, then we participate in the redemption of the human spirit. And that, after all, is what it's really all about."[4] Ideas can help us navigate this time of transition and create new visions.

THE TRUTH ABOUT CREATIVE PROCESSES AND PEOPLE WHO EMBRACE THEIR CREATIVITY

Let's look more closely at this notion that creative people are lazy and waste time in not actively working. With almost no exceptions, the highly creative people I have met are disciplined. They pick up an instrument or a paintbrush, get themselves to the dance studio and begin to warm up, set appointments to collaborate with others, and persevere at generating ideas until something comes to them. They have some sort of regular mindfulness practice that quiets the chatter of the analytical brain and awakens the parts of the brain involved in creativity. You might say that when they seem to be doing nothing, they are actually doing something very important: working with the brain and their mind state to prime themselves to experience high levels of creativity.

Everyone stops to gaze at the sky or smell the roses to some extent. But when Henry David Thoreau took long walks through the woods near Walden Pond, he came up with the book *Walden* while someone else might emerge from the forest with no fresh ideas, having spent their time ruminating unproductively. If you want to avoid that and make your downtime work for you, establish a mindfulness practice and learn from the stories in this book about valuable mind-sets and habits that can prepare you to achieve creative breakthroughs.

Another myth people have heard about creatives is that they are depressed, mentally unstable, or both. Creativity has many benefits, including increased happiness and decreased depression and anxiety. While some studies have connected creativity with a higher rate of bipolar disorder and depression, the vast majority of studies show no connection and, in fact, demonstrate that creative people are *less* likely to be mentally ill than people who are out of touch with their creativity.[5]

Research has shown that the key brain difference between very creative people and others is having more neural connections among different systems within the brain. Highly creative people are able to activate and use these systems simultaneously, which contributes to their innovative abilities.[6] It's possible that some people are born with more of these connections, but it's likely that all of us can develop them regardless of how talented we might think we are.

However, if you do have an emotional/mental disorder, a mindfulness practice—something I strongly recommend to all my clients—can be extremely helpful for managing it. One of my highly creative clients who has bipolar disorder, and who was taking prescribed medication for his condition, was leery of meditating, as he feared it would reduce his creativity as a designer. I asked him to try it for a short time, and if he found that it made him less creative, I wouldn't push him again. He also wanted to reduce the dosages of his medication routines as he increased his mindfulness practice and to increase his number of therapy sessions from one to two times per week. I agreed as long as his prescribing physician was on board with the plan. To my client's surprise, after making these changes, he found that he was just as creative as before he began mindfulness practice. But now, instead of experiencing manic highs, which had him filling notebooks with ideas that yielded few true gems, his moods were more even and he was writing less, but the ideas he was recording were of far higher quality.

This creative artist was far from the only one I have worked with who had to be coaxed into letting go of the false belief that treating his mania would rob him of his creativity. If you have bipolar disorder, depression, anxiety, ADHD, or another mental health disorder that involves different brain chemistry, be sure to read chapter 8, "Meditation, Medication, and Psychedelics." As the son of a man who struggled with bipolar disorder, and as someone with a history of anxiety attacks, I feel strongly about helping people who suffer with mental health disorders acknowledge their unique experience of their illness and partner with professionals to tailor their treatment so they can harness the power of their creative gifts.

IT'S NEVER TOO LATE TO BECOME MORE CREATIVE

Another myth people subscribe to is that we automatically lose creativity as we get older. We've all heard of late bloomers who hit their stride creatively after midlife. Frank McCourt, who taught English at high schools and technical colleges, wrote his first book when he was in his mid-sixties: *Angela's Ashes* (1996), his memoir about his impoverished upbringing in Ireland, won a Pulitzer Prize and became an acclaimed feature film. Ken Jeong was a twenty-nine-year-old physician who worked on his comedy act until he got his first big break as a comic actor in *The Hangover* at age forty. If you're afraid it's too late to become highly creative, recognize that creative people may simply have developed and sustained habits of thinking differently—something you, too, can choose to do at any age.

You can also consciously decide to look at situations from new perspectives and be less defensive when you're challenged to think differently.[7] It's important to consider the context of people's behavior rather than negatively judging them and dismissing them as wrong, odd, or bad. Stopping to consider where they are coming from will be easier to do as you practice mindfulness. That's because mindfulness develops the area of the brain associated with self-awareness and reduces the density in the right amygdala, part of the brain's emotional center and, specifically, the part associated with immediate responses to stimulation. In fact, the participants in a 2010 study called "Meditation and Changes in the Right Amygdala" scored lower on a perceived stress scale even as they showed these brain changes. Meditation leads to changes in the right amygdala.[8] We also know that as little as half an hour of mindfulness practice a day for eight weeks can measurably reduce amygdala density according to research carried out by Sara Lazar and her team at Harvard University.[9]

Training your brain to be calmer and less emotionally reactive develops what I call mindstrength: the ability to control your responses to people and situations, remain clear-headed, and begin to steer the energy of strong emotions or exuberance in a direction you choose. Anger, excitement, or despair can be transformed into a creative force. Even so, you can come from a place of happiness, well-being, and enthusiasm and experience creative breakthroughs—and what Mihaly Csikszentmihalyi in his groundbreaking book *Flow* (1990) called creative flow. I call it the download of core creativity.[10] My experience working with highly creative people has convinced me that people tend to underestimate their ability to adopt more flexible, creative thinking and reduce the influence of any biases that blind them to valuable new ideas.

One of those is the bias of having a fixed rather than a growth mind-set. A fixed mind-set is the belief that talent is more important than persevering at building skills. A growth mind-set is the belief that what matters is working hard and smart toward your goals. A small business owner I know says she is not a natural salesperson but has done a lot of research, adopted new ideas about marketing, and honed her skills to the point where she now enjoys this essential business activity. She's not afraid to admit where her skills and knowledge are lacking because she has had a lot of practice at refining them. She's an example of someone who, like many creative artists, has adopted a growth mind-set and habits for resilience, innovation, and reinvention.

If you think about your own potential for transformation and success in achieving new goals, be honest with yourself about your beliefs. Examine them. Do they indicate a fixed mind-set or a growth one? Are you willing to develop a growth mind-set and to be open to greater possibilities for yourself?

It's never too late to develop new habits of thinking, even if the adult brain is less malleable than a child's. While studies seem to show creativity reduces as we age, researchers from Columbia University and New York State Psychiatric Institute who looked at the brains of people up to age seventy-nine found that "healthy older subjects without cognitive impairment, neuropsychiatric disease, or treatment display preserved neurogenesis"—that is, they maintained the ability to grow new brain cells. The researchers also said, "It is possible that ongoing hippocampal neurogenesis"—brain cell growth in the part of the brain related to memory and decision making—"sustains human-specific cognitive function throughout life and that declines may be linked to compromised cognitive-emotional resilience."[11]

Dean Keith Simonton, a distinguished professor of psychology at the University of California at Davis, who has extensively researched and written about creativity and aging, found that "[t]he precise relation between age and creativity depends on the domain. Some creative types—such as lyrical poets and mathematicians—tend to have early peaks and relatively rapid declines, whereas others—among them, historians and philosophers—are prone to later peaks and gradual, even negligible declines."[12] And if you're concerned about health, wellness, and well-being as you grow older, there's good news: mindfulness practice benefits your heart, reduces cellular aging, and supports a healthy, robust immune system.[13] Creativity can improve immunity, too.[14] And participating in visual arts such as sewing, sculpting, and painting produces changes in the brain that may be protective against stress in later years, according to a 2014 study.[15] These creative activities might even prevent dementia, say some researchers at the Mayo Clinic. The theory is that creating new neural connections in the brain protects its health.[16]

NEW PERSPECTIVES

I have found that even people in their twenties can be out of touch with their creativity. They struggle with divergent thinking—the ability to come up with multiple ideas—often because it hasn't been fostered in them. That said, I once told a creativity and mindfulness workshop group of millennials at Snapchat in California that it's important to "think outside of the box." They said, "What's this box we're hearing about? We don't work in boxes. We interact with each other. What do you mean?" The image stuck with me. You might not recognize the boxes that confine you, but everyone has some. They can provide a sense of security, but breaking out of them can be extremely rewarding, helping you create a vision for yourself that's more in sync with what you most want to experience rather than what you think you should desire. That ability to imagine something new is crucial for all of us because of the changes we're experiencing.

Some believe that teams can't be creative or productive unless they're in a room together, so people must spend their workdays in offices for the creativity to flow and people to remain on task. A better way to think about the current mix of working in offices and remotely is to recognize that even if workers are able to return to open-space offices completely at some point (and many workers hated this type of setup anyway), there might be an advantage to changing how teams work together remotely and in physical space. Zoom and similar software apps weren't on anyone's radar twenty years ago, but now we can't imagine life without them.

What ideas could you come up with if you were bold enough to acknowledge your confining "boxes" and start imagining ways to break out of them altogether? What breakthroughs might you experience if you allowed yourself to "play" with new ideas? I've seen enough everyday people do this to confidently say that whatever you think your limitations are, you can find security in relying on a creative process instead of remaining stuck in constricted ways of thinking, perceiving, and operating. Cynicism and pessimism can be huge obstacles when you're trying to adjust to changing circumstances.

Children and teenagers are more oriented to novelty than are adults. The adolescent brain is wired for risk-taking and novelty seeking—key aspects of creativity. As adulthood approaches, adolescents often feel the pressure to set aside their creativity and follow a narrow, formulaic path to success as it is defined by their family and culture. Creativity is often deprioritized, relegated to an evening or weekend activity. Yet as Buddhists say, the wheel of fortune is always turning. Impermanence is the natural state of life on Earth. Why wait for life upheaval to foster and develop the creativity that can help you achieve greater equanimity, resilience, and optimism?

WHAT HAPPENED TO YOUR CHILDHOOD CREATIVITY?

It's unfortunate that myths about creativity and pressures in our younger years keep so many people from accessing their creative abilities. Sir Ken Robinson's TED Talk "Do Schools Kill Creativity?" has attracted over 71 million views, in part because many people sense that any creativity they had as a child vanished along the way to adulthood.[17]

When I was in a private Boston Catholic school (grades 2 to 5), the art class and music class were very rigid and tightly designed. In art, we were told what to draw and what paints to use, and in music, we were taught to read music and pick one instrument to focus on, in a very classical way. When my family moved me from that school to the public school, the art teacher I had in junior high used to say, "What paint colors do you see and feel connected to? What are you feeling inside of yourself today that would show up best on the canvas?" And before we would start the assignment, we would meditate: she told us to close our eyes and go inside and use our imaginations.

Simultaneously, I had a wonderful music teacher whose classroom had many types of instruments—guitars, a piano, an organ, drum sets, horns, you name it. He'd ask all the students to go outside the room and imagine playing the various instruments. Which would we like to try? We would go in, pick one up, try it out, and then, every fifteen minutes, switch to another one. It was extraordinarily freeing. That same music teacher would have us listen to classical, rock, folk, and jazz music, and I credit him for turning me into a lover of many forms and types of music. The broad background in music I developed as a result of having that teacher was invaluable years later when I was working with musicians in a variety of genres who came to me for counseling or coaching. When people want to change direction, I get that. I understand that even if you invested a lot of time and energy into following one path, there can come a point where you're ready to change. I tell my clients, "Don't be afraid that your brain can't learn, that it can't rewire itself." Anyone can open up multiple creative pathways in thinking and feeling, in drawing and painting, and in playing music and writing.

That marvelous sense of freedom to create that you had as a child is something that you can get back. If you feel you didn't really have it, you can get it now—and even into your hundreds. It's available to you and everyone. From a brain plasticity perspective, closed doors can spring open in the pursuit of creativity, but for this to happen, you have to let go of old notions that were drilled into you. I can remember that if I told a nun that my little brother said something interesting to me that was clearly not true, a product of his imagination, she would be sure to say, "Now, you told him that wasn't real, didn't you?" I'm glad to say I didn't! Imagination is underrated. I've seen it be the key to people moving past devastating losses and into a new state of happiness, well-being, and satisfaction. And as Einstein said, "Imagination is more important than knowledge. For knowledge is limited, whereas imagination embraces the entire world, stimulating progress, giving birth to evolution."[18]

Whenever I've interviewed highly creative artists (and I interviewed several specifically for this book), I have found that many had parents who contradicted any discouraging, negative messages about creativity they received at school. However, actor Cody Fern, who has starred in such celebrated television series as *House of Cards* and *American Horror Story*, was an exception. He said,

> The word "encouragement" is an emotional wound for me. I don't believe I received any of it, or when I did, it was scarce and most often indirect at home but never at school.
>
> When I was very young, pre-teens, I loved to draw. My father was a great amateur sketch artist and would draw dinosaurs and other creatures in letters he sent, or in Christmas and birthday cards. He was also an avid amateur watercolor artist. More by way of example, creativity was encouraged in these particular art forms. I always loved my dad's passion for his personal art projects, truly nothing grand—printer paper watercolors and napkin dinosaurs in pencil. But this was more an extension of him, not about my nurturing my creativity.
>
> At school, creativity was actively discouraged in me. More accurately, it was disparaged, mocked, and punished. Teachers always found me to be "too creative," "a distraction," "a daydreamer," "too preoccupied with fantasy." This became my report card stamp, inevitable no matter what grade I was in. In flashes of creativity, spontaneity, or my personality expressing itself, I was punished. I was isolated, made to face walls—constant detention and no leisure."[19]

He persevered, however, and as an adult, Fern learned to cultivate what I call a Creativity Support Pod: a group of friends he can call on when he is feeling blocked or insecure about his work. (You'll learn more about Creativity Support Pods in chapter 2, "Before You Say Hello, Say Good-bye.") Even if you didn't receive encouragement for your creativity when you were growing up, you can reclaim and strengthen it at any age. You can reawaken and exercise it as well as get support for it.

For me, in addition to the wonderful influence of my music teacher in junior high school, the fountain of my own creativity began to burst forth when I joined with my two best friends, who were masterful musicians, to play in a trio. Each of them was capable of playing many different instruments, and our group was always changing up vocals, harmonies, and rhythms. I spent most of my weekends hanging out in the afternoons in cafes in Harvard Square reading existential philosophy and Zen Buddhist texts, and when evening fell, I would head over to local music venues where I caught many of the great music acts of our time including Joan Baez, Tom Rush, Santana, the Grateful Dead, Bonnie Raitt, the Who, the Rolling Stones, Jethro Tull, the Paul Butterfield Blues Band, the Lovin Spoonful and John Sebastian, Leon Russell, Joe Cocker, Arlo Guthrie, and the Band. That experience exposed me early in life to art, music, and creativity being fluid, always changing, and taught me the importance of being in the flow so that you create something truly inspiring and powerful.

I have a friend who works in a creative field who says that she never thought of herself as particularly creative or a creative type until she took an online quiz about strengths and "creativity" came up at the top of her list. She believes her creativity was nourished by parents who weren't involved in fine arts but who deeply valued a variety of perspectives and instilled in her and her siblings a sense of curiosity about a variety of people and ideas. Trips to cultural events and institutions, family discussions about people from different backgrounds from her own, and encouragement to read books and take classes in areas outside of her comfort zone were a part of her upbringing. As a result, she became very comfortable exploring fine arts and being creative in her approach to problem solving and understanding other people. While she's the only one of her siblings to have ended up working in the arts, all of her brothers and sisters take creative approaches within their own less "artistic" fields and have been able to be resilient as changes were forced upon them by unseen factors. She says that her sister, who worked in research and development in a technology company, once had an idea for a device that would be the size of a book but would hold many books digitally, allowing someone to carry their books with them. This was about fifteen years before e-readers were invented. Unfortunately, like so many stories, in this one, the person who came up with a great idea didn't follow through on bringing it into manifestation! Elizabeth Gilbert wrote about this phenomenon in her book *Big Magic* (2015), describing a very specific idea she had for a novel that she had abandoned. Later, she met a woman who had written a novel that was uncannily similar in plot and setting. The idea had come to the woman soon after Gilbert had set it aside—perhaps unconsciously lifting it from the ether.[20] David Seltzer, who early on in his career was an uncredited screenwriter on *Willy Wonka and the Chocolate Factory* (1971) and who went on to write *The Omen* (1976) and *Shining Through* (1992) and direct several movies, said, "It is more than a coincidence that when I come up with an idea that I think is the first time anybody ever thought of it, I'll find out that eight other people are doing the same damn thing."[21] He believes there may well be a collective unconscious, as pioneering psychologist Carl Jung called it, where ideas that haven't yet taken form might originate (something I'll discuss in greater detail later in this book).

To reclaim your creativity from the past, any losses have to be acknowledged. This way, you can avoid repeating mistakes of the past and finding yourself in the same old situations. All change and transformation requires allowing yourself to grieve and feel your sadness so you can move on to experiencing excitement, joy, and enthusiasm as you begin to create anew. In the next chapter, you'll learn ways to experience and express any stuck emotions you might have.

Chapter Two

Before You Say Hello,
Say Good-bye

After a loss, you might think you're feeling good, ready to tackle the next chapter of your life. However, you might not have fully processed your emotions about what happened. People commonly retain old, hidden fears, resentment, anger, grief, and frustration. That causes them to unconsciously create situations that bring up those challenging emotions again. Sigmund Freud called this the repetition compulsion.

Feelings of sadness accompany any loss, even if the loss is part of a larger life transition that is overall positive. If you've ended a relationship or sent your youngest son or daughter off to college, if you've been let go from your job or had to adapt to changes like working from home, or if you've experienced any other significant loss, it's possible that you've resisted fully feeling your emotions and letting them go.

One sign that you might have grief or disappointment to release is being stuck in nostalgia, continually negatively comparing the new to the old. Another sign is that you're repeating old mistakes, seeking out familiar situations, because you are drawn to repeating the past instead of opening up to new possibilities for yourself in the future. Your compulsion to get back to the old ways might be mostly or completely unconscious. You don't want to wake up one day and realize you have re-created a situation that wasn't working for you or fallen back into old habits you wanted to replace.

To release old emotions you've been holding onto, you can do a simple mindfulness meditation, setting the intention to let your feelings appear in your awareness, be expressed, and subside.

MEDITATION GUIDELINES

Before doing any meditation in this book, turn off your distracting devices (such as your cell phone) and get into a comfortable sitting position on a cushion or chair. You might feel comfortable placing your
hands on your knees with your palms upward and open and possibly
touching each middle finger to the corresponding thumb to form a circle, or you might prefer to have your hands in your lap or palms down
on your knees. Set a timer so you can be sure you do the meditation for
10 or 15 minutes—whatever you decide on—so you don't start thinking
about how much time has passed, which will distract you. Then, close
your eyes—or if you're anxious, focus on a spot on the wall or a natural
view outside of a window you sit in front of—and begin.

After your meditation, rub your palms together to generate some heat
and then place them over your eyelids for a few seconds. Then, take
them away, open your eyes, and look around the room to slowly reenter
an ordinary mind state of beta consciousness, "grounding" yourself so
you don't feel lightheaded.

If you're worried that an important idea or insight will come to you
during mindfulness meditation, I encourage you to keep a journal and
pen nearby. You will probably find that you don't need to stop your
meditation to record the idea after all. You can write it down afterward
and note any thoughts or feelings you have as you look back on what
occurred during your meditation.

In fact, as part of self-reflection and mindfulness practice, and as you
learn to release old, stuck emotions, you may want to keep a creativity
journal: a notebook you write in when you want to remember what you
experienced when practicing mindfulness or in a state of core creativity
when the ideas are easily flowing for you. You can capture snippets of
ideas here that you don't yet see a way to fashion into a plan of action.
You can also use your creativity journal as a place where you work out
your understanding of your creative process as well as your emotions
and thoughts. As you do the non-writing exercises in this book, it can
be helpful to not only record your experiences but also to come back to
them later to see if you have any new insights into them.

At the end of your meditation, take a few moments to ground yourself, that is, to shake off any lightheadedness. You might want to stretch
and wait a minute before resuming everyday activities.

If you're very uncomfortable with feelings that arise during a meditation and you can't seem to shake them off quickly after ending the session, sit quietly and allow them to shift naturally. If that doesn't work,

do some physical activity to get them out of you: run, take a walk, punch a pillow, do some heavy lifting, dance, do household chores, and be mindful of the physical sensations you experience as you let the energy of the emotion move through you and out of you.

What follows is a Simple Mindfulness Meditation that I suggest you do for 5 to 10 minutes at first and the build up to 15 to 20 minutes a session and, ideally, two sessions a day. It will take practice to sustain your awareness on your breath and not let it wander, so be patient with yourself. Keep in mind that by practicing at refocusing, you're retraining your brain to be more focused. A more disciplined mind will serve you well as you strive to become more creative, so commit to regular practice.

SIMPLE MINDFULNESS MEDITATION

While in your meditative sitting position, focus on your breath as you inhale and exhale. Notice the sensations as you naturally and easily draw in the breath you need and effortlessly exhale. When a thought comes to mind—maybe you'll realize your nose itches or a dog is barking in the distance, or you'll think, "I don't know if this mindfulness meditation is doing me any good or if I'm doing it right"—don't judge yourself. Simply refocus. The refocusing is the work that builds mind-strength, retraining your brain just as repetitively lifting weights builds muscle strength.

As you meditate, you might notice sensations or emotions or both arising. While you focus on your breath, observe what's happening. Let yourself cry or feel a surge of energy or a wave of emotion if that's what happens naturally. Whatever comes up from the unconscious, let it express itself.

End your meditation when the time is up.

In time, with practice, you will develop the ability to remain fully present in the moment more easily—even if you experience strong, challenging emotions that come up. You'll find that, like everything else, they are impermanent. They will move through you if you learn to surf them. Notice them, but keep refocusing on your breath.

Mindfulness employs attention to the breath, concentration, and inquiry into the body-mind process. Other forms of meditation, such as Transcendental Meditation™, are similar in that they involve a simple focus—in TM, you work to retain your awareness on a mantra, a Sanskrit word you keep repeating to yourself silently. Herbert Benson, of the Benson-Henry Institute for Mind Body Medicine at Massachusetts General Hospital and a Harvard Medical School professor emeritus, reported in his book *The Relaxation Response* that repeating an English word such as "one" or "oneness" achieves a similar response.[1] Much of the research on meditation has focused on mindfulness meditation and practice, but it's possible that focusing on a mantra rather than your breath would be as effective a sitting practice as mindfulness meditation is.

OPEN MONITORING MEDITATION: A VARIATION ON MINDFULNESS MEDITATION

In addition to mindfulness meditation, you can do open monitoring meditation, which I would argue is a form of mindfulness meditation. To do it, you remain focused and mindful. However, instead of sustaining your attention on one thing (your breath or a mantra), you sustain it on your experiences in the present moment while breathing naturally and relaxing into sensations, emotions, memories, and thoughts as they arise. You broaden your focus to all of these experiences.

When doing open monitoring meditation, maintain your attention on the present moment and all that is unfolding, even if what's happening is a thought appearing in your mind. When something happens, simply notice it and acknowledge it as an anxious thought or the sound of thunder in the distance, to give two examples. What you don't want to do is start running with that thought as if you had climbed upon a wild horse that will take you wherever it wants to go. Simply note the thought and then refocus on the moment, remaining present in it. Refocusing on your breath, feeling yourself inhale, exhale, and pause before inhaling again, can help you stay off that horse.

Some research and anecdotal evidence suggest that open monitoring meditation makes it easier to come off the meditation cushion ready to dive in to divergent thinking, that is, coming up with multiple ideas and ways to solve a problem.[2] However, in my experience, over time with practice, mindfulness meditation alone can quiet the ruminating and negative self-judgments that make it difficult to tap into core creativity. You may find yourself focusing on your breath and then noticing a thought arising, remaining present with it, and feeling a sense of excitement. Remain with that experience and notice what else unfolds. You might tap into core creativity and experience a big "aha" moment. If you like, you can choose to begin a mindfulness meditation session and then allow yourself to experience open monitoring. If you're one of the many people who struggle with any sort of focused meditation, however, you might decide to stick with mindfulness meditation alone when doing the ten-week Core Creativity Program. Should you decide to try open monitor meditation for some of your mindfulness meditation sessions, you might want to make note of whether afterward you find it easier to brainstorm ideas than if you hadn't meditated or if you had done mindfulness meditation.

WHY MINDFULNESS MEDITATION IS SO HELPFUL

Mindfulness (or open monitoring) meditation will help you increase your awareness of what is happening in the moment, develop greater insight and wisdom, and ultimately achieve an open mind state. In open mind, which you'll learn more about in chapter 5, "Absorbing Creative Stimulation and Getting into Open Mind Consciousness," you can access core creativity, experiencing creative flow as well as your intuition and inner wisdom.

What does it feel like when you shift into open mind and begin to feel core creativity download? Actor Cody Fern says, "Sometimes I have to pull the car over when I'm driving. It feels like something is being born in me, something big is coming. The creative moment and the future are meeting." His advice? "Be open to what it wants and to follow it or to not follow it. Don't force or careen it into a direction. This process is about allowing, trusting, and seizing the creative moment before it moves on. You have to drop everything and just *go*. It seizes you and it commands you—not the other way around."[3] Core creativity is powerful, so you want to work at being able to get into a state of open mind.

As you develop mindfulness on your meditation cushion (or chair), you will more easily practice it in your life, applying it to everyday activities such as brushing your teeth, having conversations, and doing your work. In this way, you're living mindfully and priming yourself to experience the flow of core creativity. You're not letting an endless string of thoughts, many of which might be worrisome, block you from experiencing a state of openness to new ideas and possibilities. (You'll read about multiple ways to enter a state of open mind in chapters 5 and 6.)

If you are a leader, manager, or owner of any organization, you'll benefit greatly by practicing mindfulness and then by promoting the practice organization-wide. Mindfulness practice will help with conflict resolution, encourage feedback sharing, and promote creative problem solving.

The mindfulness practice we use today—where we focus on what is happening in the moment, usually while sitting and meditating—is an outgrowth of the ancient Theravada school of Buddhist meditation known as Vipassana (or "insight") meditation. First taught in India around 2,400 years ago by Gautama Buddha after he attained enlightenment, this relaxing and brain-rewiring practice was brought to the West and popularized in the twentieth century by many yogis, swamis, gurus, and teachers such as Jack Kornfield, Lama Surya Das, Joseph Goldstein, Sharon Salzberg, Roshi Joan Halifax, Jon Kabat-Zinn, and Tara Brach. There are many types of meditation, but I find that mindfulness meditation is like rocket fuel for self-awareness and developing greater creativity.

Sometimes, my clients are concerned that doing meditation will violate their religious beliefs as non-Buddhists. I tell them about Thomas Merton, a Trappist monk and author of many books on Christian mysticism and meditative prayer. Merton was a strong proponent of Christian contemplative prayer but also meditation. In fact, he spent the last years of his life in India and in Southeast Asia studying and practicing Vipassana meditation and befriending the Dalai Lama. Other Christian contemplative mystics who studied and practiced meditations include St. John of the Cross, St. Theresa of Avila, and Meister Eckhardt. If you're unsure about whether mindfulness meditation violates the teachings of your religion, you might want to discuss it with a spiritual leader. However, mindfulness meditation as I write and teach it is secular, free of any religiosity.

I urge all my clients—and you—to establish a mindfulness meditation practice. Sit for two 10- to 15-minute sessions a day at first, as I suggested, but ideally, push yourself to do two 15- to 20-minute sessions. If you're too restless to sit, you can exercise beforehand to see if that helps. Consider doing mindful movement, too, such as yoga, tai chi, or qigong for example—or even walking. My friends Rob and Tracy Donnell, who attended some of my mindfulness meditation and yoga workshops, came up with the term "yogatating" to describe what they do: 5–10 minutes of yoga stretching followed by sitting for 20 minutes in mindfulness meditation.

Practicing in nature lets you take advantage of one of the best benefits of nature: time outdoors in a natural area cues your sympathetic nervous to turn off its response of fight, flight, or freeze (primitive and reactive responses to perceived danger), which might be chronically active due to stress. As your body reduces its levels of the stress hormone cortisol, your parasympathetic nervous system takes over and relaxes you: your brain cues your endocrine system to release hormones that alleviate the grip of stress, lowering your blood pressure and heart rate to normal levels.[4] If you can't meditate outdoors in a natural space, you might do it indoors while listening to nature sounds from outside or a recording.

If mindfulness meditation proves difficult for you despite these strategies, you can start doing mindful walking for one of your two mindfulness practice sessions each day. When possible, do your walking meditation outdoors in a natural area, even if it's just your yard.

MINDFUL WALKING MEDITATION

Begin your mindful walking practice standing up. Focus on your breath and how your abdomen rises and then falls as you naturally inhale and exhale.

When you feel centered, make a fist with your left hand and cover it with your right, and then place your hands at your navel. With your eyes open fully, looking down at the ground, slowly shift your weight to your left foot as you lift your right foot, and say to yourself "lifting." Pay attention as you move your foot forward, and, as it touches the ground, say silently, "placing." Perform the same slow motion as you step with your left foot, remembering to think "lifting" as you lift it and "placing" as you place it on the ground. You might find it takes concentration to keep your balance because you're moving as if in slow motion.

As you continue mindfully walking, make mental notes about any thoughts, feelings, sensations, sounds, smells, or even tastes that you notice as you remain focused on your breath and the practice of lifting, shifting, moving, and placing. If you realize that your mind has wandered, bring its focus back to your walking meditation. Do this as often as needed without negatively judging yourself. It can take practice to sustain your focus.

Continue until you've done mindful walking for 15 to 20 minutes.

In the days after September 11, 2001, in New York City, I was teaching a workshop at the New York Open Center. After I had the participants do a brief mindful sitting meditation, some shared that they had trouble keeping their eyes closed: too many horrific images from that day were coming to them. I suggested that the next time they meditated, they sit with eyes open looking ahead at something that has a particular color or image that is comforting—maybe the sky or the clouds—to free their minds from the disturbing imagery that was coming up for them. Or, I said, do walking meditation with your eyes open, and I showed them the practice. Most of these survivors and witnesses reported feeling relief from not having to do sitting meditation with their eyes closed and felt that, ultimately, walking was easier as a mindful meditation practice than the sitting practice. So, while I would like you to try mindful sitting as one of your two daily practices, if it turns out to be too challenging for you even with your eyes open, go ahead and do mindful walking or mindful movement of some type instead.

WHY MINDFULNESS PRACTICE
HELPS YOU SHIFT EMOTIONS

Our emotions don't linger if we allow ourselves to feel them. Mindfulness practice helps you to shift out of feelings and moods—if you have the physiological foundation for experiencing and sustaining emotions such as joy and excitement.

Mindfulness practice awakens what's known as the witnessing or observing self, a facet of your consciousness that observes what you're experiencing. There is the self who is immersed in the intensity of feeling and emotion and the experience you are having (such as a verbal argument), but there is also the self that is noticing the event unfold and how your anger or frustration feels in your body. The witnessing self gets awakened in mindfulness practice. In time, you'll be able to rely on it to step in and create a space between you and your emotions when you are feeling overwhelmed.

As if taking your pulse at intervals throughout the day, stop for a *mindful pause* so you can observe what you're experiencing. Mindful pauses let you tune in to what's important and what's not, making it easier for you to remember to let go of what is unimportant—or unwholesome. In Buddhism, we talk about wholesome, neutral, and unwholesome thoughts ("wholesome" means "supporting well-being"). If you're not aware of your mind's internal chatter, you might not realize how many of your thoughts are, at best, neutral and, too often, damaging to your sense of well-being. Taking mindful pauses can help you become conscious of the quality of your thoughts, giving you the opportunity to consciously replace them with ones that are conducive to feeling equanimity, tranquility, and optimism. You might even want to set aside a day to practice taking mindful pauses: set a timer to go off every hour to remind you to tune in to what you're doing rather than letting your mind wander. Or, use sticky notes to post reminders to yourself to take a mindful pause: affix them to spots in your home or office that you come into contact with often such as light switches, windows, and doors. Whenever you encounter them during your day, stop and take a mindful pause. Notice what's happening, and ask yourself the following:

What am I feeling now?
What am I sensing now?
What am I thinking now?
Am I having the type of experience now that I want?

If the answer to the last question is "yes," take a mindful breath and savor the experience. If not, ask yourself, "Where does my attention and awareness need to be refocused for me to feel that I am in a zone of calm and openness to creative flow?" Mindfully redirecting your awareness provides you with the opportunity to reset your compass.

Let's say you're in a conflict with someone. If your observing self is active, you might notice tightness in your muscles and a desire to forcefully voice your opinion even as the other person is talking. At the same time, your witnessing self is able to silently say, "I'm frustrated." Then, you'll find yourself thinking about what you want to do next. Being aware of your emotions and not trying to repress them allows you to experience that you can tolerate them for a time before they shift—or before you consciously do something to change them. For example, you might envision them taking form and then seeing this form grow smaller and smaller until your emotion feels manageable. Think of a sailboat sailing away from you toward the horizon, growing smaller and smaller, or a ball of anger or anxiety that begins to shrink until it is small enough for you to throw into the distance.

Because it activates the witnessing self, mindfulness practice can train your brain to alter any habitual resistance to feeling your emotions, making it easier for you to experience them and observe as they transform, naturally flowing and shifting like the currents of a river. And over time, being able to access your witnessing self when you're upset develops your ability to be less emotionally reactive and have less intense reactions as well. That allows you to be more adventurous and creative, more open to experiences that might not be pleasant but could be valuable. If you often avoid your feelings after a loss, mindfulness practice is an excellent remedy for that afflictive habit.

Director and screenwriter David Seltzer happened across the witnessing self naturally and told me in a conversation, "I think there's always a piece of me that is not solidly here, because I'm constantly aware of where this conversation could have gone and didn't, and what I might say. . . . The way most conversations go is people jump in whenever they get a thought. It's the witness in me that enables me to withhold, because I'm really watching the dynamic. I know if it's something important, it will come around in time. But I'm watching this like it's a little scene that I don't want to destroy by tampering with it too much. So I'm known as a good listener." Listening is an excellent skill if you want to be creative, as it's part of absorbing new stimulation and ideas generated by others. Of course, it's also a great skill to use in your personal relationships, too.

MINDFULNESS AND CREATIVITY

Cultivating your witnessing self as a result of mindfulness practice breaks you out of viewing external reality from a rigid, fixed perspective, loosening you up so you can be more creative. As you become more observant of your thoughts, feelings, sensations, and behavioral patterns, you're able to witness your inner nature and how your mind works. It becomes easier to experience a quality of spaciousness and equanimity because your mind is freed of the excess debris it churns up—worries and distractions that take you out of experiencing the moment. Being more mindfully present lets you see with new eyes and hear with new ears. You've observed many sunsets and walked on the same sidewalk many times, but when you have cultivated your witnessing self, you more easily pick up on what you never saw before. Cynicism falls away as fresh insights and ideas come to you. There are only seven notes on a musical scale and eighty-eight keys on a piano, yet pianists continue to create new melodies, confident that there are tunes yet to be written.

Mindfulness also improves your focus, helping you to be more productive. While the creative process always involves generating some ideas that go nowhere, mindfulness can amplify any that come to you, giving them more color and vividness. That's because mindfulness allows you to access the resources of your creative unconscious from which core creativity flows. It's important to respect and trust images and insights that appear during mindfulness practice or shortly afterward because they are emerging from the zone of core creativity.

Mindfulness can help you overcome insecurities about your creative abilities. As Ellen Langer, a professor of psychology at Harvard University and author of *Mindfulness* and *On Becoming an Artist,* says, "The more mindful we are, the less self-conscious we are. The more we know just what we're going to do before we do it, the more opportunity there is to be self-conscious and to proceed mindlessly."[5] When a musician is improvising, in the flow of creativity, the areas of the brain associated with self-consciousness are not active. Thoughts such as "Maybe what I'm creating isn't very good" don't form.[6] Also, mindfulness practice helps you recognize when you're feeling insecure and address that feeling consciously by choosing to hold more positive beliefs about yourself and your potential.

OTHER BENEFITS OF MINDFULNESS

As if all those benefits weren't enough, mindfulness meditation has even more to offer you. It reduces your stress and the production of lactic acid, which causes fatigue, and the stress hormone cortisol. Over time, high levels of that lead to cellular inflammation and illness. Mindfulness meditation also increases your levels of interleukin and supports a strong immune system as well as the cleansing of toxins that can affect your mood. These physiological changes enable you to switch off the sympathetic nervous system and switch on your parasympathetic nervous system, as described earlier.

Also, meditation enables the practitioner to shift out of a beta brainwave state (associated with everyday consciousness) and into states of alpha and theta (associated with relaxation, being in a trance, and accessing deep creativity). Over time, practice at switching into higher frequency alpha and theta brainwaves helps you get the restorative rest your body needs for cellular repair, making you get higher quality sleep even if you're getting less sleep than you were before.

After establishing a meditation practice, you might find you regularly wake up feeling refreshed and revitalized instead of groggy. Sleep disturbances and depression are correlated, and depression can dampen not just your mood but your creativity and resilience after a loss—another reason to make sure you're meditating after a loss or whenever you're having sleep issues.

Meditators often report a more enhanced and heightened state of colorful dreaming as well as feeling that their intuition is being awakened and even improved. While the benefit of that might not be obvious, many creatives throughout history have experienced breakthroughs as a result of dreams. Nineteenth-century scientist Michael Faraday discovered the structure of the benzene ring after dreaming of two snakes biting their tails. Author Robert Louis Stevenson, who wrote *The Strange Case of Dr. Jekyll and Mr. Hyde*, received crucial ideas for his plot when scenes came to him while dreaming. And Paul McCartney dreamed the entire melody for "Yesterday," a tune so perfect that at first he was convinced that someone had already composed it and that he simply had remembered it while asleep. He has said, "For about a month I went round to people in the music business and asked them whether they had ever heard it before. Eventually it became like handing something into the police. I thought if no one claimed it after a few weeks then I could have it."[7]

For all the reasons I have just given you, I strongly encourage you to try mindfulness meditation. Feeling your emotions can be uncomfortable or even painful, but if you block them, you can become stuck.

ACKNOWLEDGE YOUR LOSS
SO YOU CAN MOVE FORWARD

Often, people underestimate the impact of a loss on them—and in particular, their mood and their creativity. Acknowledging what they've lost and expressing their feelings and observations can help them say good-bye to the past and open up to the possibilities available to them in the present.

In the early 1980s, I was hired as a creativity consultant by the Walt Disney Company to work with their Department of Imagineering, which included top-line filmmakers, designers, executives, directors, artisans, and producers who had been involved in designing and constructing features in the Disney parks including the Epcot Center, which had just been completed. I wasn't surprised to learn that many reported that while they were excited and proud of the result of their teamwork, they simultaneously felt a sense of loss. Epcot had been the last part of Walt Disney's vision to come to fruition, and there was a strong, shared sense of an important chapter of the Disney story ending. My job was to do workshops and trainings on how to move forward into cultivating a new vision. To help them with this process, I knew I had to get the team to acknowledge the loss that comes with the completion of a project and let it go.

Some of the people I worked with were caught up in perfectionism, wanting to tinker with something they had completed and that the top executives had already signed off on. It was like John Lennon's admission to an interviewer who asked if there were any Beatles songs he wished he could go back and change in some way: Lennon said, "I'm dissatisfied with every record the Beatles ever fucking made. There ain't one of them I wouldn't remake . . . including all the Beatles records and all my individual ones."[8] However, John Lennon went on to write more songs after that and didn't go back to rerecord his earlier ones. I needed the Disney team to enter a new chapter and begin creating again instead of looking to the past and holding onto it.

I encouraged the team to express what they were experiencing. One said Epcot felt like a memorial and that she felt she was mourning the past. Some team members felt an abiding sense of aimlessness because they didn't yet have a new goal. Others said they were having trouble sleeping due to an uncomfortable sense of restlessness. I knew that voicing their emotions and thoughts would help everyone see that they weren't alone in having mixed feelings and even some anxiety about the path forward. Knowing they weren't alone was part of the process of releasing emotions and thoughts that could become obstacles to creativity.

I suggested that we all look at the loss as a creative challenge akin to when a world heavyweight like Muhammad Ali lost a fight. We would have to remain in shape to get out there for the next fight. I taught about the need to look at endings as beginnings: the closing of a chapter might lead to a renaissance.

I led the team in a meditation that returned their minds to the initial thrilling experience of working on a large project—back to the days when Epcot was still just Walt's idea that had yet to take form, with the Imagineering team deep in the process of envisioning how it might look. I also led them to reexperience in meditation everyday triumphs and exciting moments, such as when they had come up with a new idea or felt themselves in a state of happiness and enthusiasm as they worked on a small aspect of the Epcot project. I told each of them to keep a journal by their side as they revisited these moments of creative flow and draw or write what came to them in meditation.

I also used the following Perfect Completion exercise with some on the Disney team I worked with who were perfectionistic and felt frustrated that they couldn't fix what they saw as flaws in the final product of Epcot. The visualization trains the brain to feel a sense of contentment that would come if a project had actually been perfected (or completed if it was left unfinished). It may seem strange that a visualization could trick the brain into creating a sense of perfect completion, but it can. You can also use this meditation to envision yourself completing a project you had to end before you felt a sense of closure.

Over the next six months as I worked with the Disney Imagineering team, I had them practice mindfulness, going deep within to observe what they found there. I explained that they should observe their moods and feel their emotions, riding waves of sadness and loss that would ultimately give way to the flow of new creativity. I said that in loss, there are always new ideas as well as solutions to problems. Sometimes, you have to say good-bye to the old to make space for the new. To do that, people need to take time to rest and refocus. Rushing to figure out the next big goal can be a problem.

PERFECT COMPLETION VISUALIZATION

Begin in a meditating position, and then focus your awareness on the space between your eyebrows, which in yogic traditions is the gateway to the intuitive, creative mind. This "third eye" chakra or energy center is what you want to use for envisioning: it is where your pineal gland, where you generate the hormone melatonin—which causes dreaming when you sleep—is located. It's helpful to focus on this energy center whenever you're trying to envision something new, which you'll be doing in this meditation.

Now remember back to a time when you wanted to complete a project or bring closure to a situation but were unable to. Re-create in your imagination how you felt, what you saw and heard, and any other sensations that you experienced at the time.

Now imagine that you are the writer and director of this movie. You can insert a new scene with a preferable ending. Do that in your imagination. Notice how you feel as you do this and once the scene is in place. Remain present with the satisfaction of a perfect completion to the experience. In your imagination, draw the positive energy of your emotions of happiness and satisfaction into your body, placing it where you sense it would be good to anchor it, knowing you can draw on that energy again when you are feeling frustrated or dissatisfied.

End your visualization when you are ready.

We often spoke about the need for each person to reset their own mind and allow a new vision for themself to begin to form so that the entire team could begin to imagine a new future. Being a highly creative and multitalented group, they met my suggestions with very little resistance. They were eager to shift into a creative mode. Acknowledging the loss and doing the meditations I suggested helped them release any emotional detritus standing in their way.

Sometimes, you'll find you're resistant to letting go of something that used to be exciting, enjoyable, and fulfilling for you but is no longer. It could be a relationship, a creative project, or a job you have outgrown. Knowing when it's time to move on is easier if you practice mindfulness.

The greater the investment of time, money, and emotion, the greater the attachment to the hope that it will pay off despite evidence that it won't. As it becomes increasingly clear that it's time to bail from the situation you're in, your ego's fear is likely to push you into denial and try to prevent you from reflecting on whether you should cut your losses. When you've adopted creative habits and mind-sets and are practiced at entering open mind, it's easier to both invest in the development of new creative work, a new self, or a new organization and to accept your losses. You'll have much more faith in yourself and your ability to discover and create new opportunities, access new ideas and insights as well as resources, and not get stuck in pessimism, grief, or anger.

If you practice mindfulness, you'll more quickly recognize and acknowledge that the outcome for your decision isn't what you hoped for and be able to change course. There's a bias called sunk cost: it's the mind's resistance to accepting that after all the time and energy you poured into a particular endeavor, it isn't going well and you need to act sooner rather than later. Without mindfulness practice, you're more likely to become ensnared in this bias and engage in avoidance behavior.

If you have sunk-cost bias, you might also find yourself procrastinating about making changes that your inner voice is telling you to make, hoping you can salvage your situation—procrastinating about moving on and accepting the loss. You might also fear it's too late to make a big change. However, growing older and experiencing the passage of time might also help you be more conscious of how you would like to use the time you have left. You might find you're better able to break out of your complacency and remain true to your values and priorities than you were in the past. At any age, you'll find that mindfulness practice helps you catch yourself when you're resistant to changes you know you need to make.

THE POWER OF GUIDED VISUALIZATIONS

In addition to doing mindfulness practice and adopting the mind-sets and habits of very creative people, I strongly encourage you to do the guided visualizations you find in this book. They are excellent tools for helping you shift out of the feelings and thoughts you have from the past and into a new experience, because your brain responds to an imaginary experience as if it were an actual one. When using guided visualizations, you're employing your imagination to cue your brain to feel what you would like to feel or experience something you haven't actually tried out yet. In a sense, you're acting, creating a reality in your body. Actor Cody Fern says that when creating a character, he uses sense memory to reexperience emotions that are familiar to him, saying he needs to get "into my body. I have to experience it and then actively store those feelings. I'm always looking to dissolve the membrane between me and the character. You're living the experience by embodying it in real time."

How powerful are guided visualizations? As I said before, we know that time in nature reduces anxiety and levels of the stress hormone cortisol. Researchers decided to test whether merely imagining you're in nature has benefits, too. A 2018 study in the journal *Frontiers in Psychology* that looked at guided imagery exercises for alleviating anxiety found that participants who used guided imagery of being in nature experienced greater relief from stress than participants who used guided imagery that didn't involve nature scenes.[9]

When you do a guided visualization, engage your senses. Feel what it was like to stand in a particular room. Re-create what you saw, heard, or touched. That can make the experience feel even more real.

As you do the exercises in this book and process your losses, whatever they are, you'll also want to make use of a valuable human resource: other people who can support you in your creative endeavors. We'll look at that more deeply in chapter 4.

Chapter Three

Reclaim Your Creative Self

When you're transforming personally, it's natural to feel some resistance to change as you wonder who you are becoming and whether the "new you" is a self you'll feel comfortable with. Even when transformation seems positive, you can experience fear, loss, or discomfort with a significant change in your personal identity.

You might fear that you're becoming a "creative type," as I wrote about earlier, but what you're actually doing is reclaiming your creativity and creative self. Broadening your definition of "creative" might help you feel more at home in your new self or identity.

Creativity involves reassembling what already exists: putting together ideas that haven't been combined before. It also involves perceiving differently instead of from a default perspective. These are aspects of creativity that one client's parents had instilled in him despite their lack of involvement in the arts beyond enjoying other people's artistic expressions. As you begin your process of envisioning what comes next for you, think about what it would take for you to see yourself as a creative, innovative, adventurous, or even daring person. What would it look like for you to be more creative than you are right now? When does a writer become a writer? When he's first paid to write something? Or when he sees himself as a writer, maybe when he is a young adult writing short stories? Our identities change over time, and you may be realizing you want your identity to change. Think about how you would describe the new identity you would like to adopt.

Even if you don't resist the idea of becoming more creative, your identity—how you perceive yourself—may need to change for you to achieve transformation and begin to reach your goals. Breakthroughs that come as a result of accessing core creativity are infused with potential but remain ephemeral until you take action. If you see yourself as someone who works for others instead of an entrepreneur, or as an artist and not a businessperson, or as a businessperson and not a creative artist, your belief about who you are and who you can become might hold you back from making the moves you need to take to achieve your goals.

A friend of mine had never invested in the stock market beyond investing retirement money into an index fund and a bond fund she had set up years before with the help of someone she had met who worked in finance. One day, a friend of hers said, "You're smart. I don't understand why you don't invest more in the stock market. I'm not as smart as you are, and I've made money buying individual stocks." My friend realized that while she thought of herself as a smart businessperson, the words "investor" and "stocks" made her feel intimidated—even though technically, by having invested in a stock index fund, she was a "stock investor." Because she had grown up with some negative messages about money and her potential to earn it and build wealth, she decided to become a "stock investor." This would be a new identity for her. She felt it would help her feel more knowledgeable about making and managing money, but more than that, it would help her feel more confident about those skills. She took a small amount of savings, started an online stock trading account, and began learning about stocks and reading a business newspaper online. She also joined an online group for people learning about wealth building and discovered tips and strategies that helped her make more money. Perhaps even more importantly, her involvement in the group helped her build her confidence in having and managing money. She realized she had to feel comfortable with who she was becoming—a wealthier person who was somewhat knowledgeable about investing—to overcome guilt about being someone who wasn't living paycheck to paycheck like so many of her friends and family members did.

My friend also had to explore her fear that if she didn't hold onto her old beliefs and values about money, even if she kept her investments a secret, people she loved who had beliefs about money like her old ones would somehow sense the change in her and wouldn't like the new person she had become. When she discovered this unconscious belief, she recognized that it was an irrational fear that had held her in its grip for years, preventing her from becoming more knowledgeable and confident. It had also kept her from growing her savings, which certainly didn't benefit anyone. Her discovery made her start questioning other beliefs about money and security that she was starting to become aware of, whether it was her beliefs or other people's. Why did she feel as she did about investments and spending? Would she be happier if she adopted different beliefs? The relatively small act of risking some money in the stock market led to her developing greater confidence about her money management and her choices that conflicted with other people's.

Fear of losing other people's approval and becoming somehow less ethical, good, likeable, or honorable are just two hidden or not-so-hidden fears that might hold you back from making changes you've decided you want to make. Other fears that could be blocking you from reclaiming your creative self and experiencing transformation include the following:

- Fear that you'll become like your parent, taking on that parent's worst attributes
- Fear that your friends and family might see you as arrogant for thinking you're the type of person who could do something they haven't done before. For example, you might decide to start a business rather than continue to work for someone else—and you might fear they'll reject you for making this choice.
- Fear of being seen by others as bad because you're odd, rebellious, or different in some way because you have changed
- Fear that you aren't the type who can master skills considered essential for your new relationship or pursuit. You might have a fixed mind-set rather than a growth one.
- Fear that you won't like your new role and will have wasted a lot of money and effort achieving your goals only to be more unhappy than you are now
- Fear that if you activate yourself as a creative you will be judged and criticized for taking a risk and leaping from the familiar into the unknown
- Fear that you won't like yourself once you step into the new role (for example, being a leader and managing other people, being a committed long-term partner, being a parent)

- Separation anxiety over leaving behind what's become a familiar role (which can be particularly difficult if you've been successful or happy in that role)

Mindfulness can help you uncover these fears and anxieties and overcome them. You can also use the Day in the Future exercise to discover any hidden fears you have about change that will lead to your adopting a new identity. Pay attention to any signs that you're uncomfortable with the new you so you can explore them. You might end up adjusting your vision of who you would like to become, or you might decide to work at letting go of old fears and beliefs that are going to get in your way.

DAY IN THE FUTURE VISUALIZATION

Sit quietly, and in your mind's eye, focus on the space between your eyebrows—your "third eye," as explained back in chapter 2, "Before You Say Hello, Say Good-bye." Imagine you are able to leap forward in time to a day in the future when you are experiencing happiness, core creativity, and vitality. In this future, you are about to start your day. You'll begin engaging in activities that will enhance and bring forth a deep and abiding feeling of being at one with the moment, fully present in what you are experiencing, feeling enthusiasm for what you are doing, and comfortable doing what you are doing. On this day in the future, you no longer have to work to earn money. You are totally free to pursue your creative dreams and ambitions without pressure. How do you wish to spend this day? What are you most passionate about pursuing now that you are in this free space rich with possibility? What are your plans for the day? Do you see yourself walking in nature, picking up a guitar and playing, planting a garden, teaching a class?

As the scene of your future day unfolds in your mind's eye, take a series of mindful breaths and then imagine inhabiting your future self. Feel yourself having the experiences you're imagining. Ask this self, "What am I feeling now as I inhabit this self?" "Who is having this experience?" (In Tibetan Buddhism, you ask this question so you can project your consciousness into the future and tune in to your consciousness while you remain grounded in your present self and your body.)

Then ask yourself, "What am I sensing now?" and "What am I thinking now?"

If you feel any sense of constriction, resistance, or heaviness emotionally or in your body, ask, "What is the source of this feeling?" and wait to see if an answer comes.

Then, ask yourself, "What can I change in this scene to shift into feeling vitality and enthusiasm for what I'm doing?"

The answer might be that you want to change something in the scene, or it might be that you want to let go of your constriction or resistance for now. Imagine placing it in a box for safekeeping, to be explored later, or in a journal, where you will read about it later. Then, return your attention to the scene and yourself in it. Feel what it's like to be this future you.

Move on to the next scene of activity in this day of happiness, core creativity, and vitality. Once again, pay attention to how you feel when you are immersed in it and experiencing your future self. Continue imagining yourself in everyday scenes as you project yourself into the future, ending with the completion of your future day. Remember, pay attention to any constrictive or resistant feelings, thoughts, or sensations that you will want to explore further as you write about your experience during this visualization.

When you are ready, you can end your visualization. Or, you can imagine yourself experiencing a day even further in the future—three months, one year, three years, or more—making the same observations and asking yourself the same questions. If you're uncomfortable with moves and transitions, you might find yourself uncomfortable with imagining a future day that you experience soon after making a big move but comfortable and even enthusiastic when imagining a future day that's even further down the road. You might experience the opposite, too—bored with your new project after a short time (at least, in your imagination). End your meditation after you feel you've gained enough insights to better understand what you would be facing if you were to make a particular choice. Then write down what you experienced so you can explore what your feelings, thoughts, and sensations of constriction or resistance related to. What made you uncomfortable in the future scene or scenes? What could you do to be more comfortable in those scenes and more comfortable inhabiting the future you?

Don't judge or criticize your resistance. The famed hypnotherapist Milton Erickson viewed all resistance as creative and useful, something to be harnessed and to make friends with. Make it work for you rather than fight it or attempt to eradicate it. As the saying goes, what you resist will persist. Your resistance won't magically go away if you try to ignore it.

Do the Day in the Future Visualization again after you have explored any constriction or resistance you felt and see if you have a different experience.

BREAK THROUGH CREATIVE BLOCKS

Blocks to creativity and change can be rooted in old losses or trauma and can arise unexpectedly. That's what happened to one of my clients who was a writer who had been successful in her craft for many years but had suddenly developed writer's block.

When she came into my office, she reported that she felt as if she were inside a large block of ice and her arms and hands were frozen. She had no ideas and would stare at her laptop screen paralyzed, unable to type more than a few sentences before deleting them. After I took her medical and psychological history over a few sessions, I recognized signs that she might be dealing with unconscious trauma and abuse. I am trained in Somatic Experiencing therapy, a form of body-mind therapy invented by Peter Levine and described in his book *Waking the Tiger: Healing Trauma* (1997). This modality involves releasing trauma from your nervous systems through a process that involves applying attention to the breath so that you relax and your trauma starts to reveal itself in your movements or posture (for example, you might start shaking or hunching over).[1] The therapist then suggests movements that counteract these physical experiences, such as reaching upward and stretching if you have a defeated posture.

Smoldering in the ruins of a loss can involve very intense emotional energy, which gets bound up in the body. This often causes a blockage to creativity that is experienced as a creative block of unknown origin. Free up that emotional energy of loss—loss related to the ending of a project or situation, for example—and you can turn sadness or pain into the energy of generating ideas and crafting them. As one of the Disney Imagineering team members I worked with said, "We needed to use the emotions of loss like a diver uses a springboard"—an apt metaphor.

I knew my client had to release the pain and afflictive emotions and harness them to use in a pursuit of her own choosing and that doing this healing work could help her get to a new level in her writing—I've seen it happen with other clients. I felt confident that Somatic Experiencing work would help my client liberate herself from her creative block. As we worked together, I had her meditate and focus on her "blocked" feeling. Where did it reside? What were its qualities? As she identified the blockage, her shoulders rolled forward, and she bent in on herself as if she were frail and frightened. She began talking about when she had been molested by a family member, a memory she had not retrieved for many decades. As we worked together, she began to have dreams of scenes from her screenplay, and upon waking, she felt renewed and eager to work. Soon, her writer's block began to melt away.

My client's story illustrates that sometimes a feeling of being stuck in a rut—a block—can be connected to something deeper that our unconscious needs to attend to. Toward the end of our therapy, as my client was writing again, she told me that it felt as if the ice blocks had melted and become streams and rivers of beautiful words.

Mindfulness practice and mindful movement can help you discover insights that might include past trauma, and you might be able to release the emotional energy related to trauma by using these techniques. Bessel van der Kolk, author of the groundbreaking book *The Body Keeps Score: Brain, Mind, and Body in the Healing of Trauma* (2014), wrote, "Traumatized people chronically feel unsafe inside their bodies: The past is alive in the form of gnawing interior discomfort. Their bodies are constantly bombarded by visceral warning signs, and, in an attempt to control these processes, they often become expert at ignoring their gut feelings and in numbing awareness of what is played out inside. They learn to hide from their selves."[2] For this reason, he says, "it is critical for trauma treatment to engage the entire organism, body, mind, and brain."[3] Emotions don't just reside in your brain. You experience them in your body. Even if you don't feel you've experienced a trauma, emotions can get stuck energetically in your body.

Where does mindfulness come in? As van der Kolk has written, "Mindfulness not only makes it possible to survey our internal landscape with compassion and curiosity but can also actively steer us in the right direction for self-care."[4] Mindful movement can help, too—that's the basis of Somatic Experiencing, a therapy I mentioned earlier. And van der Kolk has done research showing yoga can be as effective as, or even more effective, for healing PTSD as psychotherapy or psychopharmacology.[5]

Many people find it difficult to access their emotions. They feel numb or minimal emotion even when in a situation that we would expect would cause a strong emotional reaction. One way to get in touch with your emotions is through exposing yourself to the arts. Go to art museums and galleries, concerts, and comic or dance performances if you can, but also find online sources of art whether it's on social media, a website for a museum or artist, a site for artistic photographs of nature, or something else. You might also want to sit back, turn off any devices that might interrupt you, and listen to some music that will take you on a deep journey inside yourself, whether it's music with lyrics or instrumental music. Do mindful listening, paying attention to your emotional and physical responses to the experience. What if any thoughts come up? Notice them and consider having your creativity journal by your side to write down your impressions or sketch them out during or after the session.

You might also watch a film or read a book that inspires you to self-reflect. When it's difficult to access your feelings or unconscious beliefs, you can often bring them into your consciousness as a result of doing these activities. You might find yourself tearing up over a piece of music or when reading a passage in a book and decide to explore why you were so moved. Did a forgotten memory resurface? Did you connect with an aspiration you set aside long ago? If you start to cry about a book or movie character's emotional pain, you might find you're ready to reflect on your own emotional pain, having released some of it through crying.

Some emotions might make you uncomfortable or even cause you pain as you experience them, or you might fear or resent them. If very uncomfortable emotions or sensations arise as you're engaging a work of art, take deep, slow breaths, and exhale slowly as well to cue your parasympathetic nervous system to become active, relaxing you as the emotion moves through your body and your stress hormone levels drop.

From the perspective of self-awareness and self-care, there aren't any "negative" emotions. Anger, resentment, and fear all can have valuable messages. Grief can remind you of how much you loved and valued someone or something, but you also don't want to get stuck in sadness and depression or any other emotion you've already learned from. You can explore your emotions in depth, learning about the multiple causes for your irritability or anger, but then you will want to release old emotions because they're simply the detritus of old experience with no new insights for you to glean from them. You don't want them to hold you back and cause you to resist transformation. That's when the Body Observation Meditation can help, as it allows you to discover where your emotions are stuck energetically in your body and need to flow, with help from your intentional choice to cause them to move out of you.

BODY OBSERVATION MEDITATION

Sitting comfortably, focused on your breath, relax into a state in which your mind's chatter has lessened and you feel present in your body.

From focusing on your inhalation and exhalation, switch to focusing on the top of your head. Become aware of this part of your body. Notice any sensations that arise in your awareness as you remain focused on the top of your head. Pay attention to the qualities, whatever they are—heavy, soft, warm, cold, sharp, dull, fluttering, tight, constricted, blocked. Notice any emotions that seem to be present here in your body at the top of your head. Then, as you inhale, imagine you are breathing in cleansing energy you can send to that region to alter it so that the sensation or emotion changes to one that is more pleasant and wholesome, making you feel lighter and more optimistic. Continue breathing this cleansing energy into the top of your head until you feel a transformation in the emotions or sensations.

Once you have done that—or if you observed no sensations or emotions when focused on the top of your head—draw your awareness to your neck and shoulders. Again, if you are experiencing no emotions or sensations here that you want to transform, shift your awareness to a lower part of your body—your chest and arms, and later, in sequence, your abdomen, your belly, your pelvic region, your legs, and your feet. Whenever you notice a sensation or emotion you want to transform, intentionally direct your breath to that area to bring transformational energy to it.

Continue until you feel cleansed of all unwholesome sensations or problematic emotions. In this way, you rid yourself of the energy of any emotions that are no longer helping you in some way.

Note: You might also try doing this exercise with an alternative way of releasing the emotions (and any sensations related to them) that you discover in your body. For example, you might imagine a hand made of warm, loving, healing light penetrating your body, grasping the sensation or emotion and gently pulling it out of you. You might also visualize a fluffy, warm bath towel wrapping around you and drawing out the sensation before being whisked away and a new one taking its place, wrapping around you, ready to towel away any more sensations or emotions you wish to have removed from your body.

Also, if during the Body Observation Meditation, you discover emotions or sensations that are wholesome and energizing, perhaps because you anchored them there in the past, you can enjoy experiencing them. What's more, you might find that they stick with you after the meditation, making it easier to avoid self-doubt.

I recommend doing the Body Observation Meditation often, especially if you tend to compartmentalize your emotions or stuff your feelings, or if when doing the Day in the Future Visualization you felt resistant to embodying your future self. Using the Body Observation Meditation in conjunction with the creativity journal and other exercises in the book can help you discover and move past blocks, which in turn can keep your emotions and creativity flowing.

Then, too, you might find that by framing your situation differently, the block dissolves by itself. Director and writer David Seltzer says,

> As a writer, I think you're being protected by writer's block. There's something that you don't want to acknowledge or has been sitting quietly for too long. The voice is saying, "Take a breath, take a breath. You're going off on a tangent here. You don't really know what step three is going to be now that you're doing that." And I say, respect a writer's block as though it's your best collaborator. Give it time. Listen to it. Take a walk. But don't think—don't feel—that you've created this. You haven't created the writer's block any more than you've created your talent. It's a gift. Accept the block. Talk to the block, and you will find your way out. Don't say, you're my enemy, I don't want to know about you, I'm going to write anyway. No, take a breath, it's your talent telling you that you're not doing as well as you should. That's my experience of it.[6]

RELEASING YOUR BLOCKS

Whether you're experiencing a creative block or not, you might want to do the Return to the Scene to Change It Visualization. Once you've discovered the origin of the block, by returning to the scene of origin in your imagination, you can change the scene in your mind, removing the block. (You might want to do the meditation more than once for an even stronger effect.)

One of my clients, Jayla, who is a musician, came to me because she was feeling blocked in her creativity. She also told me that she was experiencing severe frozen shoulder and was having difficulty playing the guitar.

RETURN TO THE SCENE TO CHANGE IT VISUALIZATION

Sit comfortably, close your eyes, and focus on the sensations of inhaling and exhaling. Continue until you feel the thoughts in your mind have quieted and you are open to wisdom from the core.

Imagine yourself going back in time to the moment when you first had the thought you have identified as an unwholesome and negative belief about yourself. The thought may have been something like "I am not creative," or "I don't deserve to have what I want for myself." Wait for a memory to arise in your consciousness. Observe where you are and the details of the setting. Is it a room in a house? A park? What are you doing?

Observe whether someone is speaking to you. What is the person saying to you? Who is this person? Was it a parent or your brother or sister? A teacher or classmate? Whose voice is it?

Listen to the sound of that person's voice. How does it feel to hear what is being said to you? Notice any sensations in your body—maybe a tightness, or heaviness. Notice *where* you feel this sensation—it could be in or around your heart or around your head. You might feel it in the energy around your body and in your body. Just observe it and keep focusing on your breath.

Remain present with this feeling as you observe the scene. Notice whether the scene or your experience of it changes. If you would like to end the visualization now and contemplate what you learned, go ahead and open your eyes. If you would like to go on to change the scene in your imagination, continue by directing the scene to unfold in a more desirable way. You can imagine others in the scene, or yourself, acting differently. End the meditation when it feels right to do so—perhaps after you feel a shift energetically or emotionally or both.

After you open your eyes, pay attention to how you feel. Less resistant? More creative? You can repeat this visualization as often as needed to dissolve any blocks you have been experiencing.

We did the first half of the Return to the Scene to Change It Visualization, and Jayla recalled being in a music class at school. Her music teacher frowned at what she was playing and turned down her guitar amplifier. "That's when I first started doubting my talent," she said. She told me she heard the teacher's voice telling her to stop playing the riffs that were flowing out of her fingers, because they were "annoying."

I asked her how she felt reliving this moment as she returned to the scene where her creative block originated, and she said, "Constricted." We talked through how she had internalized the teacher's voice to some degree and whether it had been triggered recently. Jayla said she had listened back to a new recording she had made and had been unhappy with her playing. Becoming conscious of the origin of her insecurity and recent creative block helped her feel less constricted.

Then, using Somatic Experiencing methods, I got her to stand up and to bend her knees, relax, and breathe deeply and breathe more deeply before picking up her guitar, which I'd asked her to bring. I suggested that she imagine she was standing in front of her old music teacher again and the teacher was saying, "Yes! Give birth to this wild new sound you are creating!" I had her scream the words while she was playing and singing with spontaneity. Jayla felt she could stand up tall and noticed the pain in her shoulder was now gone. Now she was wailing on her guitar with abandon. Soon after that, she had a breakthrough in her songwriting and playing.

A few years later, when Jayla felt she had reached a plateau with her career and needed a breakthrough, I asked her to bring her guitar and amp to our therapy session again so we could revisit the visualization and this time change the scene. Jayla felt a contraction in her body's energy as she relived this moment of being in front of her music teacher. She realized that experience from long ago was still affecting her in some way.

I told her, "As you visualize the scene, I want you to imagine that one of the members of the band you were in at the time is there with you in the room, saying something positive about your playing." That scenario matched up with some actual memories of being supported by other band members, so she eagerly agreed. During the exercise, Jayla imagined her old teacher saying, "Those are some interesting riffs," and then her old band mate was suddenly in the room, saying to her, "I love what you're coming up with—it's raw, jagged, psychedelic!" The teacher nodded and said, "Yeah, that's a good way of describing the sound," and flashed Jayla a thumbs-up. Instead of feeling a sensation of restriction as she did this exercise, Jayla said, she felt excited and liberated.

I then suggested she plug in her guitar and start riffing. She was just about to play when I said, "Stand up. Feel the floor supporting you and grounding you." I knew this physical experience might help her feel in her body the confidence that she'd experienced in her visualization. Jayla got up from her chair and began playing, the music flowing from her fingers. I said, "I love what you're coming up with" and leaned over to turn up the volume. I watched as her expression and body posture changed, reflecting that she felt strong and free to express herself and give in to the flow of her unique inner music. After that therapy session, her songwriting and playing reached new dimensions, culminating in an invitation to rejoin her old band, which she took them up on. Together, they created a brand-new album and developed a new sound.

Once you identify the origin of an old belief about not being creative enough and use a visualization to trick your brain into releasing it, you can anchor a new positive feeling state into your body's energy. The constricting, unwholesome beliefs will fall away; you can experience what you need to feel in order to enter the space of open mind, where you can receive a core creativity download.

While reclaiming your creative self and breaking through blocks can be work you do on your own, you can also aim to get help from others who will support you in your desire to access core creativity and achieve breakthroughs in any area of your life. Let's look next at collaboration with a Wisdom Council of Support and a Creativity Support Pod.

Chapter Four

Support and Collaboration

Working through your fears and any anxious, pessimistic beliefs frees up energy for creativity. Getting support for your efforts can help enormously, which is why I suggest forming both a Wisdom Council of Support and a Creativity Support Pod. They have some similarities, but the first is more like a list of people you can call on while the second is a group that meets regularly—in person, if at all possible. You'll likely be collaborating with people in both groups to some degree, so later in this chapter, I'll offer you some strategies for collaboration that can help you make the best use of your human resources.

You're likely to have a Wisdom Council of Support already even if you don't call it that: you might have a mentor and colleagues who can offer insights and suggestions. You probably have friends who know you well and will be honest with you about not just where you're getting in your own way but also what you're doing or have done that's worked well for you. Maybe there's someone in your life who will tactfully point out when you seem to be sabotaging yourself, someone who will remind you of your strengths and past successes, and someone who inspires you because of their enthusiastic optimism when it comes to your potential. It's good to have people you can call on to

- collaborate with you on creative projects,
- help you get out of any rut you're stuck in,
- assist you in breaking out of a creative block,
- offer you ideas and information you hadn't considered,

45

- serve as resources or guide you to them, and
- hold you accountable for following through on your plans to achieve specific goals.

When you turn to others you know for ideas, insights, and support for a creative project, whether it's reinventing your life after retirement or writing your first novel, you might find your current "council" lacking. You might want to think about adding some of the following:

- new peers
- mentors, teachers, and tutors
- professional coaches and professional mental and physical health care providers
- people who add diversity to your council because they're older, younger, or from a different walk of life

Let's look at each group in detail.

NEW PEERS

People who are in a situation similar to yours, and who are seeking transformation, can help you see that you're not alone in experiencing confusion, insecurity, or obstacles. They can also help bolster your confidence. Together, you can share any new resources you've discovered and hold each other accountable for the goals you set for yourselves.

If you'd like to expand your list of peers who can provide wisdom and support, try to find people who can help you become stronger in areas where you're weak. For example, if you're not good at writing, you can look for someone to help you create a business plan and perfect it before approaching an investor. You'll want to connect with some people who complement your strengths but who also can encourage you to take some risks and develop new skills. Sometimes, you might simply want a peer to steer you toward someone you can hire to fill in the gaps in your own skill set.

If you're introverted, shy, or have social anxiety, you might want to set a specific goal for developing new peers and then role play with someone how you'll begin a conversation and bring it around to exchanging contact information. I once coached a real estate broker who was having trouble getting leads to sell homes. He had recently moved, had almost no local connections, and was naturally shy. I got him to commit to a goal of striking up conversations and giving out a minimum of three business cards a day. Within the year, using this model, he had sold several multimillion-dollar properties as he moved from quiet and shy to reaching out to everyone that he met.

MENTORS, TEACHERS, AND TUTORS

Mentors, teachers, and tutors can be invaluable allies when you're beginning a project or undergoing change. That said, teachers and mentors can inspire you tremendously—and so can other creative people. Painter Ronnie Landfield, whose artwork has been featured in sixty-five solo shows and whose paintings are in major museums, says,

One evening in early February 1966, I went to watch a Warhol film at the Cinematheque Theater. . . . When I returned to my studio after the movie, I saw fire trucks in front of my studio building. My studio building burned down, and I lost just about everything. . . . I got angry then, having lost so much of my work, and so I started to draw every day. I had no money, but then I got an idea from reading *Conversations with Artists* by Selden Rodman: I wrote a letter to Philip Johnson, the world-famous architect, who I didn't know, but I'd read that he was an art collector. Philip Johnson invited me to meet him in his office . . . [and] suggested that when I make some new art, I should come back and show it to him. He told me that to become an artist is a wonderful but challenging idea, worth the effort. I left the meeting inspired and hopeful. . . . Within a few weeks, I had a new studio that I shared with my friend Dan Christensen, and I had a job at an advertising agency. Within a few months I finished the series of fifteen nine-foot-high and six-foot-wide paintings as well as three more nine-by-six-foot paintings and nearly a dozen other smaller works. I went back to see Philip Johnson, and he bought one of my new nine-by-six-foot paintings. I was nineteen, and I was just blown away that this major art collector bought a piece of my artwork.[1]

You might feel you can handle challenges on your own, but why not get some help, even if it means swallowing your pride and admitting you're lacking some skills? Several years ago, I did leadership coaching with an executive at a large firm who had received an offer for a promotion. I knew Kim (not her real name) resisted adopting new technology, and for months, she had dismissed my concerns, certain that she could get away with being stuck in her analog-world ways. I sensed that her technophobia was rooted in fears that she couldn't achieve mastery and would embarrass herself.

I coaxed her for months, but Kim was stubbornly resistant. Finally, I warned her that she wasn't just risking her job but her career if she remained inflexible about developing her technology skills. Shortly after that, she told me she had been contacted about an even better position at a larger company, and during the interview, she was grilled about her understanding of digital data management. While she felt she handled the questions well considering how little she knew, she at last accepted that she had to upgrade her skills. Kim was offered and took the new job but felt insecure. She didn't know how to get up to speed with technological advances that were changing her field. She admitted to me that she needed help.

I suggested she ask to work with the company's IT expert for a few hours weekly. Additionally, I said, she should hire a tutor to work with her one-on-one in her home. This way, she would relieve some of the pressure to hide how little she knew about digital data management. Kim had no idea where to find a tutor to serve as a new member of her Wisdom Council of Support, and I told her that she should talk to everyone she knew in the city where she worked to see if anyone had a recommendation. (Nowadays, she could ask someone through social media, but back then, it didn't exist.) She found someone through a gym she began working out at, one that she suspected was attracting people who were more tech savvy than the people who exercised at the stodgy gym near her home. With the help of two new Wisdom Council of Support members and peers she found and began to meet with once a month, she moved past her resistance and became far more adept and knowledgeable than she had imagined she could be. Now, years later, she's the head of a company known for its excellence in digital data management. She even teaches online seminars on leadership and how to manage digital data. In the future, if she were to be pushed out due to ageism or some other reason, she could expand upon this side gig she had created for herself. I feel certain that if I had told Kim years ago that she would be known for her expertise in digital data management, she would have scoffed at the very idea.

My client's resistance was coming from fear of being a slow learner, so having a private tutor in addition to the company's IT expert to help her was key. With the rapid pace of change in the world, all of us are going to have to be lifelong learners, called on to build new skills and expand our knowledge bases. Any fear you have of being left behind by people who seem to learn faster than you do can be addressed by committing to finding teachers and tutors who will respect where you are in the learning curve and work patiently with you.

If you're not tech savvy, or you are but know you have holes in your knowledge and skill set, you might need to address that. Increasingly, it's not just creative performers who are having to work on camera instead of before an audience; it's people from all walks of life who are doing Zoom calls and recording videos. And as technology continues to evolve, it will affect you. Gaining technology skills can help you do research, too, connecting you with teachers, mentors, creative tutors, physicians, psychotherapists, and peers. And if you're tech savvy but socially awkward, think about getting help to smooth over rough patches in your communications and interactions with people.

Taking lessons from a skilled teacher can lead to big leaps in your mastery and your understanding of the topic as well as get you to think more deeply about what you're doing, which can lead to breakthroughs. Musical composer and steel drummer Jonathan Scales, who has recorded seven albums, was strongly influenced by a musical composition teacher and steel band director who taught Jonathan in ninth grade to explain why he wrote the things he wrote: "He might say, 'Why did you write this? Why did you put this here?' And it wasn't to belittle me. It was to get me to show my intention. . . . The only wrong answer would be, I don't know. . . . He really taught me to have intention in everything that I write."[2]

PROFESSIONAL COACHES AND PROFESSIONAL MENTAL AND PHYSICAL HEALTH CARE PROVIDERS

Sometimes, it's hard for people to be honest with us even when we ask them to be. Sometimes, people we know don't have the professional expertise to give us the insights we need to work through very difficult challenges. Consider adding professional coaches and professional mental and physical health care providers to your Wisdom Council of Support. They can offer objectivity and professional insights that others on your council might not be able to. They can also help you hone your plan for reinvention, as they'll likely have resources you don't know about and much practice helping other people who are going through a personal transformation.

As a psychotherapist and professional coach, I'm glad I underwent counseling myself years ago when I was a young intern working at a student mental health clinic at my university. I had an older and wiser supervisor named Dr. Seymour Cabin, a clinical psychologist whose previous position was on staff at the Yale Psychiatry Department Clinic in New Haven and who had worked at the Austen Riggs Psychiatry Institute in Stockbridge, Massachusetts. During a supervisory session I had with him, I presented a case of a young man whose father was jealous and highly competitive with him. Dr. Cabin could tell I had rage and fury in my voice and suggested that I talk out the emotions about the case with a therapist. At first, I was resistant. I didn't want to believe there was anything "wrong" with me, but Dr. Cabin went on to share that he saw a therapist weekly. He said that his mentor in psycho-analytic training had taught him that if you want to become a master at therapy and remain aware of your countertransference (how you get triggered by your patients' issues), have a good supervisor but also a great therapist you see weekly.

I took up his suggestion. Through therapy, I came to discover that I was holding onto anger at my father that had bled over to my work in the university clinic, making me identify with the other student who had father issues. I recognized that my father's criticism of my choices— including my choice to study psychotherapy—were the result of jeal-ousy: he'd felt he was locked into his career choice at an early age. That helped me let go of my anger at my dad and feel compassion toward him. While I wanted to consider myself an expert therapist, letting go of my anger and undergoing therapy myself not only helped me but made me a better therapist.

My experience undergoing counseling set me on a path of deep psychological transformation lasting four decades. I have continued to seek out support during times of crisis, loss, change, and personal and professional decision points. I feel it's essential for therapists to undergo therapy themselves to better understand themselves and how their psychology affects their work with their patients.

I have coached therapy clients outside of therapy sessions but warned them that coaching and therapy are quite different. Therapists work with emotions as they help patients uncover patterns and address them. A coach is most useful when you are not dealing with family of origin or developmental issues and you want someone to help you set goals and keep you on track, providing accountability so that you don't slip into avoidance behaviors. I tell my coaching clients before beginning this aspect of our work together that if they expect to experience my warm, empathic counseling style when I am coaching them, they should just focus on their therapy needs.

The best way to find a good therapist or coach is to identify people in your personal or professional life who seem successful according to your definition of success, have an evenness of mood, a calm temperament, deep compassion, good listening skills, and a healthy attitude toward taking risks. Then, ask them if they are seeing or have seen a therapist they can recommend. Ask them, too, if they have attended any seminars, summits, webinars, or workshops that were not only educational but inspired them to take positive action they might not have taken otherwise. (See the resource section at the end of this book for ideas.)

Ask your doctor, nurse practitioner, or other health care provider for a recommendation, check your insurance company's list, and compare these recommendations to listings on the *Psychology Today* website if a recommended therapist has a listing there. You can search online for details about a therapist's background and how they work, but you can also call and ask about a consultation. You can also research therapists or coaches by searching the internet for "therapist" or "coach" plus other terms such as "mindfulness," "creativity," and so on—and your location (such as "Los Angeles" or "Omaha") if you're not open to tele-sessions. But keep in mind that the very best resources are your friends and colleagues. If they admire a therapist or coach, be sure to ask them why. What they appreciate in a therapist or coach might be very different from what you want.

In your initial phone call, discuss with the therapist or coach why you're seeking therapy or coaching. Ask whether they have undergone therapy and, if they're a coach, if they have undergone coaching. If they say no, my advice is to keep looking.

Ask any prospective coach how they work and what their training is. I recommend that you start by looking for someone with a certificate from a program such as the College of Executive Coaching, Coach U, the Coaching Institute, or the Canfield Coaching Institute. There are other coaching schools, too—check a school's website "About" page to be sure you feel comfortable with the level of training certified coaches have received. Take a look any particular coach's client testimonials, too.

Note that some professional coaches are also therapists or social workers who can assist you in navigating between the world of emotion and the realm of envisioning and taking action. Also, pay attention to whether you get an indication that the therapist or coach has biases that make you uncomfortable. There are even diversity and inclusion coaches that can make you uncomfortable—deliberately!—to get you to recognize your own biases that are affecting you and the people you're interacting with (for example, as an entrepreneur, teacher, or leader of an organization).

If you're interviewing a therapist, ask what theoretical operating systems they use that they might employ in your treatment (such as mindfulness-based or somatic approaches). Some therapists are rigid and use only one or two approaches. Some limit themselves to talk therapy and don't address the body or spirituality. Some focus more on the past than on resolving your current challenges. Think about how you feel about those focuses and limitations.

My own feeling about therapy is that when someone's fallen down a deep hole and needs help getting out, my job is to extend them a ladder rather than dig deeper within that hole, uncovering more and more problems and issues they might want to address at some point. I like to start with what is most concerning them at present and have them experience some successes before discussing other problems that they might become aware of as part of the therapeutic process or coaching. I find that focusing on strengths and self-actualization shines light on potential pathways for personal transformation.

In addition to a therapist or coach, your Wisdom Council of Support might also include healers who will help you address challenges you're having physically, energetically, or spiritually. Pay attention to their approach. A holistic, functional medicine MD, a nutritionist, or an acupuncturist might be good members for your council, especially if you have ongoing issues they can help you address. If you feel dismissed, condescended to, or ignored, confront this person to change that—or move on. You want help from people who admit that what you're dealing with is outside of their scope of expertise and who admit to having made mistakes. Defensiveness is a bad sign. Therapists are taught to pay attention to how their own issues might be influencing their dynamic with their patients, particularly if problems result from this counter-transference. While other professionals may not receive this sort of training, it's important not to gloss over biases of theirs that make you uneasy. You want to work with people who are available, clearly committed to their work, able to self-reflect, and respectful of your values.

At any point, you might want to add or remove people from your Wisdom Council. Members may turn out to be less helpful than you had thought they would be, may become unavailable, or may no longer be appropriate to consult with for whatever reason. While you're adding or replacing members, you might want to use the Consulting a Mentor Visualization to feel supported as you embark on change. This meditation is especially helpful when you don't have people currently on your Wisdom Council of Support who are available to boost your confidence and advise you. The answers from your imaginary mentor will be coming from your unconscious, which might have more insights than you realize.

CONSULTING A MENTOR VISUALIZATION

Sit, relax, and ready yourself to do a meditation. Focus on the space above your nose in the middle of your forehead to awaken your ability to envision the perfect mentor for you.

When you're ready, imagine this mentor is sitting in front of you. Let your unconscious suggest who it is, whether it's a real person that you know (or once knew) or someone you admire but may never have met. Let their image arise in your mind's eye.

Imagine that even if you don't know this person in real life, or don't know them well, they know you and have watched you develop your skills and strengths. They will generously offer you plenty of insights, guidance, and ideas.

Ask a question of your mentor. It could be something like "What do
I need to do to open up more opportunities for myself?" or "What am
I not understanding about the frustrating situation I'm in?" or "What
could I create for myself that I haven't thought of yet?"

Picture your mentor considering your question for a moment and
then giving you an answer. Feel free to ask for further clarification and
to ask more questions.

When you are ready, imagine your mentor saying, "I'm glad you
came to me for help. I'm confident you can take it from here. I've seen
how much you have worked to get to this point. Don't worry about
achieving your goals. You've got this."

Feel the energy of your mentor's confidence entering you as your
mentor reaches out toward you, offering you this valuable gift. Anchor
the confidence within your body and energy field by silently affirming
"I've got this" as you place the energy where you feel you need it. Affirm silently, "I've got this." Feel that to be true for you in this moment.

Thank your mentor for counseling you and end the visualization.

After doing this visualization, remember, you can draw on the energy of confidence that you received and anchored within your body's
energy field—and you can use the Body Observation Meditation to feel
yourself reconnect with it.

Note that you can use the Consulting a Mentor Visualization with the
intention of having an imaginary conversation with a specific person,
maybe someone who would ideally serve on your Wisdom Council of
Support but who can't for whatever reason. Again, the answers you
receive will be coming from your unconscious, and they might contain
some important insights and ideas.

DIVERSE MEMBERS ON YOUR COUNCIL

If you are looking at the people you go to for advice, new ideas, and
insights, and they're all the same age, think about how to add to your
Wisdom Council of Support people of different generations. Diversity
among your Wisdom Council of Support members is important. You'll
want to get perspectives of people who have more wisdom and a broader
perspective than you do and people who have knowledge and skills you
lack. You'll want to ask questions of people who can see what you're

overlooking. Diversity creates the possibility of greater convergence of your ideas and reality. I like to confide in people who challenge me, and I know they operate from a completely different perspective.

I'm a boomer born in 1950 to a wild and wooly Irish Catholic family with a father who worked for AT&T for over forty-five years: he received yearly stock options, worked until he was sixty-four, and was offered a good retirement package so the company could push him out. Initially, my formula for working was to teach at a university and ride it out until my sixties, when I could enjoy a pension. When I moved to Los Angeles and, along with some other therapists and some medical doctors, started a holistic behavioral medicine and psychology clinic, some of my first therapy patients were musicians and television and film executives. Often, conflicts with others and addiction issues brought them in. I began to brand myself as both a psychotherapist and a creativity and communication consultant and coach, inventing a soup that was to their liking. I would come to learn as much from them as they did from me.

Many of the young musicians I worked with were in a band that toured, but they would also go off and play with other musicians, rehearsing and doing gigs as well as writing new music, later to return to playing with their favored set of musicians that they toured with. Their "mix and match" approach to their work inspired me. Soon, I began thinking about what it would be like if I dropped my old plan and instead took multiple teaching gigs as a part-time instructor. I realized I could remain in private practice, be a part-time university adjunct professor, do creativity coaching, and host workshops. Later, I would realize this decision helped me avoid boredom and burnout. I continue to enjoy my work thanks to the insights I gained from working with people who were a little younger than I who had not followed the only career path I knew of: work full-time for one employer, doing the same old thing over and over, until you retire.

It's not just younger or older people who can awaken you to your blind spots and unconscious biases. Even if you think you have a diverse group of people helping you out by serving on your Wisdom Council of Support (or participating in your Creativity Support Pod), you might be missing some important perspectives.

In my career, I have been fortunate to work with people in private practice, in college teaching, and in corporate America, and with people from different cultures and demographics. Early on, I was consulting for a major film and music studio in Los Angeles when a woman approached me to say, "Dr. Ron, I really love what you are teaching us, but would you like some feedback?" I had learned from Ram Dass that he always read letters and evaluations he got from his talks and teachings and what he listened most intently to was negative feedback. And he would not only read and reread the more hostile and critical feedback forms but, when he could, he would either call the people up or write to them to better understand the feedback and where it was coming from. Some of those letters turned into long exchanges he kept going until he felt he had truly processed what they were telling him. I knew that even if it bruised my ego a little to be criticized, this woman who had approached me might offer me some helpful insights, so I said, "Fire away."

She said that she loved what I was teaching—"but you're teaching in the voice of an upper-crust white male." I was taken aback but recognized that this woman had done me a favor in pointing out my bias. I took a deep breath and said, "Tell me more," and she gave me at least five examples where I had offered case examples about work that were all about men—and white men at that. In my family, we had six sisters and four brothers, but it was obvious to me that I had some of my dad's strongly embedded views that came from spending his career in a corporate world dominated by white men. My dad had always seemed to discuss men when he told his work-related stories. Rarely, if ever, had he brought up any stories about women. I hadn't thought about how his limited experience working with women at his office back in an era when there were fewer women in the workplace might have influenced the types of anecdotes he shared.

I thanked the woman for sharing her perspective and promised I would change up my teaching stories. As a result of her feedback, I now think and teach with diversity in the foreground.

You might want to set a plan for learning more about diversity so that you can more easily network and connect with people who are different from you and who might be willing to be a part of your Wisdom Council of Support and have you be a part of theirs. If you have little experience interacting with people who have disabilities, are transgender or gender-nonconforming, are non-neurotypical, or are of a different race, ethnic group, social class, or background, you can get coaching, read books, and take classes to upgrade your understanding and skills. Learn by observing them; don't expect them to teach you everything you need to know about people who are similar to them.

Even as you add new members to your Wisdom Council of Support, don't hesitate to remove members. If the well water was nurturing, go back and drink it. But if the water was tainted, don't return. A person's insights might be good, but you might feel much too uncomfortable with how they delivered them. Be aware that people who are jealous of you are likely to act contemptuous or aggressive toward you or show in their behavior, words, and body language that they are irritated by you. That can be very hard to take. What's more, their jealousy will probably lead them to give you bad advice. Find another resource. Look for Wisdom Council members who are compassionate, confident, and open to being questioned about their formulas, suggestions, and strategies if you don't understand them or they don't feel right for you. It isn't their job to tell you what to do so much as to offer ideas and insights. You'll also want them to be patient with you even if you're at the very beginning of a learning curve—and available to talk with you when you need help.

CREATIVITY SUPPORT POD

As I said, the Creativity Support Pod is a group of people who want to support each other in their creative endeavors. I was first invited to be part of such a group years ago. The idea came from corporate mastermind groups, but the people forming the group decided it would be helpful to invite creatives: musicians, writers, visual artists, and the like. The group members also felt it would be helpful to have a psychotherapist who was also a creativity coach, so I was asked to join. Meetings were held once a week, and everyone committed to weekly one-on-one phone conversations with someone else in the pod. Frequent check-ins led to more accountability because members felt they had to answer to someone who they knew was going to ask them about their weekly progress toward their goals.

Many creative collaborations came about because of the Creativity Support Pod. In one case, a television producer was reluctant to produce his idea as a television series rather than a movie. He felt that film was more prestigious, but his description of the premise and characters convinced everyone that it could do equally well, if not better, as a series rather than a movie. We also encouraged him to consider that if the series were successful, he would be set up financially to make many movies. In time, he decided to follow the group's advice and went on to create one of the most popular cable network series ever.

Creativity Support Pod members can assist each other in developing new ideas, sharing resources, and overcoming challenges and hindrances such as being in wanting mind and yearning for the excitement, clarity, and camaraderie experienced with a previous project. You might agree together to ask each other questions that prod all of you to be reflective about your processes and to bring up resources others might find helpful. You could also assemble a Creativity Support Pod around whatever it is you want to transform—your career, your financial situation, your relationships, your parenting, and so on. However, you'll want to make sure that everyone knows the focus is on creative collaboration and transformation, not venting or telling others what to do.

The idea is to gain inspiration and accountability as well as a mix of people at different levels of mastery. You need people with a track record who can model success to others and share insights and strategies as well as brainstorm. While it might seem at first that people with a higher skill level wouldn't want to participate, they can benefit from the teaching they do as they think more deeply about what they know and how they work—perhaps for the first time. They also might want an opportunity to help others, and the Creativity Support Pod can be an outlet for that.

Ideally, you'll choose eight to ten people who will meet once or twice a month for an hour or two. Keep a consistent core group, only adding new people when members drop out or start missing a lot of meetings. Decide ahead of time how often someone can skip the group before they have to decide whether to recommit themselves or move on. Maintaining a core group makes it easier to assist every member with their challenges that they bring to the group for discussion and input. My pod was composed of about a dozen writers, directors, producers, and filmmakers, and at least eight of us were at every weekly two-hour meeting for a decade. Your pod could meet less often but for a larger block of time, such as once a month for three hours.

Have the meeting at someone's home or in a public space such as a restaurant or coffee shop, and start with sitting in a circle for a group check-in. At the first meeting, go around the circle and have everyone briefly introduce themselves. One person should lead the group that week, and the facilitator should change every time you meet. The leader or facilitator should keep track of time and clarify which three individuals will have twenty minutes to present the challenge they're facing and seeking input on. Distribute everyone's contact information so people can have more discussions with other group members outside of the meeting. Encourage everyone to keep the conversations among members offline and in person or at least on the phone. It's easier for people to be vulnerable and share their ideas when they have greater privacy than they have online. Also, for many, in-person conversations flow more easily. That might be because we more easily pick up on body language when we're face to face with people in a room instead of via a screen. Some people find video meetings stressful: they might struggle with where to look and how to set up their camera in order to successfully mimic in-person eye contact. They might feel insecure about their appearance on camera as compared to in-person. If someone wants to take notes, they might feel that looking at a camera and then a notebook or keyboard is more awkward than jotting a few notes when conversing in person. New members of the Creativity Support Pod should be encouraged to pick an advocate in the group who can support them in overcoming any shyness or introversion so they can get the most out of the group.

If you'd like to start a Creativity Support Pod, take a look at who you know who might be interested in participating and eliminate from your list anyone who has difficulty working with others without dominating them or creating drama. Even if you or someone else in the pod has learned how to be the "difficult person whisperer," one domineering member can break up the entire group. Keep searching for better candidates.

My Creativity Support Pod included a few actors who wanted to break into writing and directing. We knew that more seasoned writers and directors could provide wise counsel to the inexperienced and aspiring ones. Most shows use one director fairly consistently, and the directors in our pod felt secure in their work, not competitive with those still in the aspiring stage. One day, a relatively new director was complaining about the actors he was working with and how they wanted to rewrite the script. He was challenged by a more experienced director who said, "You should listen to your actors and have them meet with the writer to talk through any problems with the script." Although the newer director had been an actor himself, he seemed to have developed amnesia about his experiences as an actor with scripts that needed improvement, and direction that was problematic for him. The more seasoned director, with my help, confronted him, asking him to remember his own experiences with directors and how he'd felt at the time. The new director was able to feel some empathy with the actors and backed down from his judgmentalism and inflexibility.

Looking at your own role in a problem can be tough on your ego, but it's necessary if you want to grow, so you'll want to have people willing to challenge you on your perspectives and opinions. The purpose of a Creativity Support Pod is *not* to reassure you that your emotions and perceptions are "right" while others are "wrong." You can feel as you do and hold onto your opinion, but you also need to see situations from other points of view and acknowledge the feelings of others you may be working with in a particular situation. You could say that a Creativity Support Pod can keep you from being stuck in one way of looking at your circumstances and letting your feelings get in the way of transformation. They can point out your blind spots and firmly challenge your resistance to learning or evolving. The more experienced director in my pod reminded the newer director that directing and acting are collaborative and asked him right out, "Is being dictatorial and authoritarian going to be your way of directing? And if that's the case, how would you have liked that if you were the actor?" It was hard for the newer director to hear, but later, he would have to admit that these forthright conversations helped him.

While we're talking about people sharing ideas and insights including feedback, be mindful that some people may be jealous and criticize you, perhaps in subtle ways. Ideally, they would not be on your Wisdom Council of Support or in your Creativity Support Pod. Check in with yourself if suggestions or insights someone offers cause you to feel anxious, ashamed, or depressed. Consider the source and the fact that all of us have unconscious biases and blind spots. Someone's harsh criticism of your plans might stem from their own insecurities or even jealousy of you. Jealousy can come out as anger, snark, irritability, or dismissiveness. Is your anxiety or shame yours or the other person's?

Also, beware of people who are passive aggressive. They will compliment you but then issue a criticism that's meant to be taken personally. After I give a public talk or book signing, often there's a line of students waiting to ask a question or make a comment. I've met enough passive aggressive people to be able to tell from the body language of a person approaching me that they're there to criticize my talk in an attempt to show off that they know more than I do on a particular subject. I can tell they want to dominate me in some way. Often, I'll say, "If you have some constructive feedback that's negative, would you do me a favor and write it down so I can read it later? I really don't want them to ruin my evening!" They're taken aback by my honesty and back off because they don't actually have constructive criticism to share, which I've exposed with my response!

Collaboration Skills

Even if you don't feel you need a Creativity Support Pod to help you collaborate, it can be exciting to feel ideas flowing as you work with others on how to solve a problem or create something, such as putting on an event or performance, writing something together such as an article or a screenplay, or starting an organization or charity. Something you feel passionate about can lead to new friendships and relationships, new job or career opportunities, and new self-discoveries.

All art requires collaborative skills—a novelist or a painter works alone a lot but also has to interact with an agent or manager, gallery owners, or a team at a publishing house, and, commonly, social media experts and publicists. And in working with peers on any type of project, being too passive and withdrawn or too domineering can be a big obstacle. You and anyone you're collaborating with has to be open to improving their ability to communicate with others. Whenever one of the Beatles came to their producer, George Martin, with a seemingly difficult-to-execute idea, he went into a creative, collaborative mode. For example, he helped them communicate their ideas to classical musicians (none of the Beatles could read musical notation). When John Lennon suggested splicing together two takes of "Strawberry Fields Forever" that were in different keys and different tempos, Martin worked with engineer Geoff Emerick to find a way to do it. Good collaborators help you find the possible rather than dismissing an idea as an impossible one.[3]

Collaboration can involve some separate work on the everyone's part, but collaborators also need to participate in generating ideas, discussing what is working and what isn't from their perspectives, and problem solving. No one wants to feel overly vulnerable or silenced, so trust and good communication are essential. While many people have the talent, skill, and perseverance to create something on their own, they might actually prefer to collaborate because when they get stuck, their partner or partners might be ready with an excellent idea. They can get help in editing and shaping as they go along and not wake up one day feeling they're completely off track, with no idea of where they're headed with their project. And they can learn from peers how to upgrade their own creative process and develop new skills. Dropping out of the "I" to collaborate, blending skills and ideas, can lead to excellent results.

Amy Ziering, a documentarian who has won two Emmy Awards and been nominated for an Academy Award, has said that she and her filmmaking partner Kirby Dick "have different leadership roles" and "different strengths." When I asked her about the team's creative process while making the movie *The Hunting Ground* (2015) together, she said, "It's sort of all blurred." I've heard that before from creative people who collaborate well: the focus is on the project rather than their individual contribution. Amy Ziering partners with fellow filmmaker Kirby Dick because he has a strength that fills in for one she lacks, and working with him is helping her develop it. She said, "I can't be effective with film if I watch it over and over again. . . . I don't become as active or attentive a viewer." In contrast, "It comes more innately to Kirby. I'm very impressed with his ability to watch something three thousand times and still be able to see it in a way that's productive."[4]

You might not recognize a challenge in your creative process until you collaborate with someone else. From there, you might feel relieved that you have someone else you can count on to make up for your weakness, and you can learn, from observing them, how to develop a new skill that might even become a strength for you.

Of course, Amy has strengths of her own. While she began her career as an academic in a comparative literature PhD program at Yale University, which many people would see as requiring verbal and intellectual strengths, she also has observational strengths that have helped her as a filmmaker. She tells this story from when she was working on *The Invisible War* (2012), a documentary about sexual assaults and how they're handled on campuses and in the military:

> We were filming a scene [with a survivor of sexual assault], and we're just trying to get B-roll with [her and her husband] at the farmers' market and walking around with their kids. And then we sat in a Starbucks just to take a break and Kirby was doing camera . . . what you see is [the sexual assault survivor] sitting down at a Starbucks and she is clocking all the exits. . . . And it's all done with her eyes just really quickly and unconsciously. . . . This is the trauma manifesting in a Starbucks on a banal farmers' market Sunday. And I didn't notice it at the time, I didn't pick up on it.[5]

But when she spotted this powerful yet extremely subtle moment in the footage, she knew to include it.

Even the most talented and brilliant people could use some help from a collaborator—and might seek it out despite feeling confident that they can carry out their project on their own. Julian Lennon once told me in an interview, "I find this collaborative process of having other talented and artistically oriented individuals listen and respond to my songs as I am shaping both the lyrics and the musical arrangements crucial to my creative process."[6] Jodi Long is an Emmy Award-winning actor who has acted on Broadway and in movies and television; she is a documentary filmmaker and a member of the board for Visual Communications and the Screen Actors Guild. She says, "Whether it is a film, television, play, or music, everything I do is collaborative. Whether it's working with a great actor, or wonderful director or musician, being with other creative people is the goal and the ultimate thrill as you jam off each other."[7]

In a culture that strongly emphasizes competition, particularly in the workplace, it's easy to find yourself resisting a collaborative process out of jealousy or insecurity. Recently, I was coaching an actor who had been very successful in her work, but after a television series she had starred in had not done as she had hoped in terms of box office and reviews, she found herself jealously obsessing over the recent successes of some of her peers in the business. I walked her through the following visualization for releasing jealousy—an emotional experience of fearing that you can't have what someone else has.

RELEASING JEALOUSY VISUALIZATION

Start with your eyes closed and palms in your lap as you sit focusing on the space above your nose in the middle of your forehead. When you are relaxed, think of something that gives you a sense of dissatisfaction, such as your job, your car, your home, or maybe your lack of recognition at work or your insecurities about your talents or qualities. You might visualize yourself not fighting for an idea you had that you believe was a good one or saying yes to a creative project that wasn't right for you. Pay attention to how it feels to experience your dissatisfaction.

Next, picture in your mind someone you are jealous of because you see them as having something you lack. Let yourself feel envious of them. Visualize their accomplishments—see them doing what you would like to do—and as you do this, notice whether you feel discomfort in a part of your body. Remain present with your feelings and any sensations you're experiencing, no matter how ugly or unpleasant they are, as you continue to picture this person's success, and continue for three to five minutes, no more.

Now visualize yourself comparing your situation to this other person's (you might picture the last time you felt envious of them). Notice what you're doing in this scene and what you're feeling energetically. Where is your energy going? How does that feel? When we project and compare ourselves to others' values and achievements, we are displacing our energy, sending it their way instead of harnessing it and directing it to ourselves for gain. Notice what you're experiencing emotionally. Does it feel good and vitalizing to compare yourself to this other person and their accomplishments, or does it feel bad, unwholesome, or even draining?

Now visualize an accomplishment of your own that caused people to praise you or made you feel proud. It's okay if you find yourself going back to childhood to remember an accomplishment that elicited these types of responses from others or from within you. The idea is to reconnect with the emotions you felt. Then, if you can, visualize another accomplishment, a more recent one, that brought you praise or a sense of pride. Remain present with this remembered experience, and then try to bring up a third experience of success and feeling good about that success. Repeating this part of the exercise builds mindstrength.

Next, in your mind's eye, see the other person's accomplishments receding to the background of your mind and becoming smaller and smaller as images of your own accomplishments get larger, crowding out and shrinking the image of the other person's successes. Do this until all that is remaining in your mind's eye are *your* accomplishments. Allow a sense of happiness as well as gratitude and fulfillment to arise in you. Notice where you experience these feelings. Your heart? Your belly? Wherever it is, that would be a good place to "store" the wholesome emotions you have about your accomplishments. With your hands, reach out to the accomplishments you see before you and pull them into your body to anchor their energy in it. When you experience jealousy or self-doubt in the future, you can draw on these emotions related to your accomplishments. They'll reside in you energetically, and you can tap into their power.

Next, visualize yourself in the future having an experience that draws praise from others and makes you feel a sense of contentment and success. Bask in this feeling. Again, you might want to reach out in your imagination to draw the emotional energy of that experience into your body and store it there.

When you have done this, end the visualization.

By using the Releasing Jealousy Visualization, you can actually feel how much more rewarding and productive it is to release your jealousy and remind yourself of your own successes than to waste energy comparing someone else's accomplishments to your own. After the visualization, the actor I was working with was able to stop her comparison game and put her energy into finding her next role.

How do you avoid becoming jealous? Author William Faulkner said, "Don't bother just to be better than your contemporaries or predecessors. Try to be better than yourself.[8] And actor Jodi Long has an attitude about competition that seems very healthy. She says, "Leave the comparisons to the others. Focus on the work at hand. Love it. Not the accolades you might get or not get. Do the work! Take the self-imposed pressure off. Be grateful you have the opportunity to do the work you love, and it will be a much more fun and rewarding journey."[9] I would add that instead of seeing others as competitors, try seeing them as collaborators. Collaboration involves not only working through your own jealousies and insecurities but appreciating what others bring to the table. You can learn quite a lot from someone who has different strengths than you do, and they in turn can learn from you.

Collaboration can be challenging when there are many people in the collaborative group, which I see often when I'm working with a team working for a company. Some team members might feel intimidated by the process of speaking up with their ideas because they're introverted, or insecure, or need more time to process their thoughts. Breakout sessions, whether in a physical space or on Zoom, are extremely helpful for supporting these participants in talking and sharing their ideas.

Also, if you're brainstorming together and you notice that someone's idea is similar to one voiced earlier, speak up so the originator is credited. While it may not seem like a big deal to you, it might be very important to them. Establishing this practice can build trust among the collaborators. Extraordinary amounts of creativity can be exchanged during the collaborative process—ideas can fly across the room very quickly, which is why recording them in some way is always a good idea. But healing can occur, too, as people who haven't had their creativity respected experience being heard and appreciated for their input.

If you feel comfortable doing so, start a creative project, however small, on your own or in collaboration with someone else. While you might think this won't contribute to your personal transformation, as I said before, I find that even just dabbling in the arts or being creative in some way can build confidence and optimism, both of which are excellent foundations for consciously fashioning a life that works for you after big changes have occurred. The project might be planting a garden, creating a short video that you might end up sharing on social media, or developing a website around a common interest you and your collaborator would like to blog about.

If you consider yourself to be creative and are feeling stuck working in your usual medium, try collaborating with someone—and also expressing yourself in a new medium. In fact, try this even if you're not feeling stuck. Painting might trigger some insights into how you want to alter your creative process as an actor. Playing piano instead of guitar or dancing instead of playing an instrument could lead to insights that improve your musicianship. You might want to take some lessons, too.

Many people procrastinate or drop projects before completing them. If that's the case for you, your Wisdom Council of Support or Creativity Support Pod members can hold you accountable for what you say you want to do but don't follow through on. You'll likely find that other members of your pod struggle with issues similar to yours and appreciate giving as well as receiving encouragement. As you begin to realize that they aren't judging you as inadequate or incompetent and can give you constructive criticism you genuinely value, it will be easier to pull yourself out of the deep, dark hole of self-doubt.

One of my Creativity Support Pod members, author Judith Orloff, known for her books on being empathic and intuitive, reminded me of a strength I have, intuition. She asked me if I would be writing about the topic in this book and sharing some of my experiences. Someone else might have been territorial about their brand and area of expertise, but Judith is confident and wants to help others; she isn't attached to her suggestions. I always know that whether I take her advice or not, she will continue to encourage me.

Similarly, my professional assistant of twenty-five years, Rhonda Bryant, will read a research request from me and ask me, did you think of going in this or that direction with the topic? She draws on her expertise, knowledge, and experience and confidently shares her ideas, knowing that I value her creative input. That's the kind of person you want in your pod. In contrast, someone who tells you that you "should" do this or that or who makes extreme statements that begin "Never . . ." or "Always . . ." probably has some baggage to work out. If you can take in their suggestions without being sideswiped by their aggressiveness or tendency to be judgmental, they might belong in your Wisdom Council of Support but not in your Creativity Support Pod. Creativity makes us vulnerable. Constantly having to dispel feelings of embarrassment or inadequacy in the face of a strongly opinionated person can shut you down, so be mindful of whether you are too often confiding in someone who squelches your enthusiasm—or too quickly dismisses your ideas.

Giving and Receiving Constructive Criticism and Feedback

If you are asked to give feedback on someone's project or idea, I find this fourfold approach keeps the conversation positive and productive:

1. *When someone is telling you about their project or showing it to you, give them your undivided attention.* Don't scroll on your phone, don't multitask, and don't interrupt except to ask for clarification. Set the foundation for them to be honest and vulnerable.

2. *Respond with positivity.* If you think it's an awful idea, you can say something like, "It sounds like you've put a lot of thought and work into this project so far." Go ahead and compliment them for their efforts rather than the outcome.

3. *Ask questions from a place of genuine curiosity.* Pose questions like, "I don't think I've heard that before. How did you come up with that idea?" and "What about this plan appeals to you the most?" Understanding where they're coming from and what their aspirations were can help you to better encourage them and give them constructive feedback. You can share what you've done in similar situations and what the outcome was. In this way, you're making yourself vulnerable and making them feel more comfortable with any criticism you offer because you're showing that, at times, you've been unsure or made wrong turns.

4. *Offer feedback diplomatically.* Finally, you can suggest something you think they might work on, but wait to see how they respond before you give them more feedback. Don't overwhelm people with criticism and advice. You can ask whether they would like more feedback or if they would rather work with their project some more first. In both my Art of Leadership and Core Creativity workshops, I'll often ask, "Would you like feedback from me mild, medium, or severe like the hottest salsa?"

Acknowledging your fears and seeking encouragement and ideas from people in either your Wisdom Council of Support or your Creativity Support Pod can get you out of the tangled net of insecurities that are constricting you, and back into creative flow. But regardless of what members of your Wisdom Council of Support or your Creativity Support Pod think, if you feel strongly that it's time to step out and take a creative risk despite their concerns, don't be afraid to listen to your instincts. Don't wait for approval, but don't dismiss the feedback you're given either.

Most people find that as they become more creative, they become more flexible and collaborative. It's easier to drop any defensiveness because they have more self-compassion and patience with themselves— and regular mindfulness meditation practice helps with that, too. Novelty and originality become more welcome in the room of self as you more easily shift into a state of open mind where you can download core creativity. That said, there are many ways other than collaboration and mindfulness practice to swing wide the doorway to the access point of open mind, which we'll look at next.

Chapter Five

Absorbing Creative
Stimulation and Getting
into Open Mind Consciousness

Core creativity and your intuition, which can offer you a rich array of ideas, are available to you when you're in a mind state called *open mind*. In open mind, you bypass the limited thinking and the biases of the rational mind, which leads to breakthroughs and intuitive insights. You experience a sense of spaciousness as your anxieties about time and your perceptions of limited options fall away, and you feel yourself open up to receive knowledge and ideas that were previously hidden from your awareness. It's as if the self who has been trying to figure out the next step has been completely overshadowed by the self that's connected to a force of creativity that stretches beyond the boundaries created by your mind. You feel expansive and, at times, exuberant, as if all obstacles have been dissolved, and you find the courage to make dramatic changes.

In his book *The Varieties of Religious Experience*, the famed Harvard psychologist William James wrote, "Our normal waking consciousness . . . is but one special type of consciousness, whilst all about it, parted from it by the filmiest of screens, there lie potential forms of consciousness entirely different. . . . No account of the universe in its totality can be final, which leaves these other forms of consciousness quite disregarded." This was one of Ram Dass's favorite quotes, and he and I would discuss open mind consciousness from James's perspective.[1]

When you have entered open mind, your natural core creativity becomes available to you instantly without effort as you lose track of time and feel deeply curious and receptive to what is novel. Singer/

songwriter/musician Paul Simon has said, "There are aspects of the creative process that [I] don't understand . . . and that's part of the great joy of it, 'cause it's a mystery."[2] He also said in a 2016 interview with Fredrik for ScavlanTV,

> I was asking a friend of mine who was a neuroscientist, "What's going on in the brain when you get into what they call *flow*?"—you know, sometimes it's described as you feel like you're plugged into the universe or the music, or the words came through you and you're just a vessel for that to happen that's so open. . . . It's happened often enough to make the career of writing songs (something that I've done since I'm thirteen) addictive. I was twenty-one or twenty-two years old when I wrote "The Sounds of Silence," and I thought, "That's good." And when I wrote "Bridge Over Troubled Water," which also just sort of came, again, I thought, "That's better than I usually write. I wonder . . ."
> It wasn't until later that I asked the question and the answer was in chemical terms: The brain secretes serotonin, which creates a feeling of well-being, and you're sort of ready to go to work and looking forward to it. And then you get a wash of dopamine and that's like the kind of "wow" experience that can be [like] either falling in love with someone or a God-like connection to the universe, something that fills your heart to overflowing. And then there's adrenaline, which keeps it going and where you say, "Gee, I had no idea it was 3 o'clock in the morning and I've been doing this for seven hours. The time just flew by!" . . . Those components seemed to be a part of what they call flow, and quite often flow produces something extraordinary. But on the other hand, there are songs that I've written . . . "Still Crazy After All These Years". . . that took me months and months of writing and changing and sculpting and all of that. And, in fact, I didn't even finish writing it until the night that we were in the studio. I wrote the bridge of the song. So there were no moments of revelation. It was just work.[3]

Actor Jodi Long says, "In my mind, creativity is not a gift. It is an extension of one's innermost being, and the gift is knowing how to access it, how to 'allow' it to come forth and then giving it to the world. It's getting out of one's head and 'allowing.'"[4] Yaro Starak, a gestalt psychotherapist and gestalt art therapist, the author of two books, co-director of the Gestalt Art Therapy Centre–Australia, and a visual artist, says, "Surrender is my guide."[5] In open mind, you aren't *trying* to be creative. You are *allowing* yourself to be, surrendering to the flow and open to receiving unexpected insights.

Experiencing core creativity that you access in open mind may result in a big idea popping into your head, or a small one that you strongly sense you shouldn't ignore. Follow that instinct! Small but important ideas can add up to major transformations, especially if you pay attention to your intuition, whether it's telling you to step back, continue steadily on your current path, or go forward with full steam.

Intuition can be invaluable for recognizing when you're trying too hard or too little to gain new ideas, form new plans, and manage the process of transformation. Best-selling author Judith Orloff explains intuition this way: "Intuition is a potent form of inner wisdom, not mediated by the intellect. Accessible to us all, it's a still, small voice inside—an unflinching truth teller committed to our well-being. You may experience intuition as a gut feeling, hunch, a physical sensation, a snapshot-like flash, or a dream."[6]

Sometimes, you intuit that a coincidence is meaningful—what Carl Jung called a synchronicity. When that happens, pay attention. I wish I had done that back in early 2008. I was in Australia teaching when I had a dream of a newspaper headline that said, "Stock market crashes. Worst crash since Great Depression." I called my stockbroker in the United States and told him I wanted to cash out of my entire portfolio. "Ron," he said, amused, "If I sold stocks every time one of my clients had a dream or an intuition, I'd never make them any money. Relax. Stop worrying. There's no way the market's going to crash."

That was the last time I ignored my intuition. It took several years for me to recoup my investment. Since then, my broker has said to me a few times, "Had any intuitive dreams lately?" (Unfortunately, the answer is no!)

You may have experienced open mind and its gifts like intuition and core creativity already. If you haven't, use meditation—but also absorption and its elements of exploring, observing, researching, learning, and tapping into your intuition using the tools of dreams and tarot cards or connecting with nature. All of these are forms of absorbing creative stimulation, ideas, and messages from your unconscious and intuition. Generating ideas and using rituals, which you'll learn about in the next chapter, can be portals, too, but let's look first at the work of absorbing.

FROM STILLNESS INTO OPEN MIND

Actor and writer Cody Fern says that for him, setting the stage to be receptive to new creative ideas looks like "silence and clearing, getting really quiet, saving the reserves of energy." He doesn't let himself think too much about how he might approach his work, which would distract him from what his non-rational brain is communicating to him.[7] Any of the meditations offered in this book, including the mindfulness meditation, walking meditation, and Body Observation Meditation from chapter 3, can take you out of overthinking and into open mind because the stillness and focus involved in meditation alters your brainwaves, and therefore, your mind state.

James Taylor said, "I grew up in the woods of North Carolina, and we had long stretches of uninterrupted—I suppose you'd call it 'boring'—time. Time to make long thoughts. . . . Consequently, as a songwriter," he says, "I crave empty time."[8] Distraction-free time can lead you into open mind as you remain present in the moment.

When the highly talented and successful guitarist I mentioned in chapter 1 said, "Sometimes, the guitar just speaks to me," he was talking about being in a state of absorption, which can sometimes happen simply by choosing to be still, observing and remaining open to inspiration—a sort of meditation. I know painters who will sit in front of a blank canvas staring at it and guitarists who will sit looking at the ocean, a guitar by their side, waiting for an idea to appear. However, they're practiced at shifting into open mind, and they find a balance between activity and stillness, between absorbing as exploration or research and absorbing as a state of being. If you have trouble getting out of your head, mindfulness practice and meditation will help. Lying in a sensory deprivation tank in the dark can be a meditation that will likely take you into open mind, too.

EXPLORING AND OBSERVING

You don't necessarily have to be completely still to enter the mind state of receptivity. Author Amit Ray, who wrote *Meditation: Insights and Inspiration* (2015), says, "Relaxed, playful, harmonious moments are the birth ground of creativity."[9] So, as an experiment, try listening to a piece of music that's very familiar to you as if you were hearing it for the first time. What do you notice that you hadn't observed before? Or, look at a work of visual art that's become very familiar to you. Open to the possibility that you missed something. Keep looking at it until you observe something new. This type of absorbing activity, in which you pay close attention and continue to do so until something new comes to you, can serve as a portal into open mind.

Absorbing can involve actively exploring stimulation—a piece of music, a painting, a film, the way a performer onstage interacts with an audience—but then entering a receptive state of open mind. Here, you "allow" as Jodi Long describes it; or as Yaro Starak said, you "surrender" to the experience. You're not in your head, thinking and analyzing. You're not forcing a download of creativity. Instead, you're letting it happen automatically and effortlessly, absorbing what comes to you.

You can find creative stimulation anywhere, but you might want to start with the arts. Cody Fern says, "I go places and put myself into situations to find the key [to unlock creativity], like going to a party to find the right person to speak with. Galleries, museums, social situations—they're situations that require me to be engaged."[10] Not long ago, I went with my friend Sophie Mollins, a noted photographer and film director, to the Tate Museum in London to view an exhibition of William Blake's spiritual art for a few hours. Afterward, when we went out for coffee, we both felt a surge of creative energy. The two of us brainstormed together about a new ending to a film she was creating and a section in this book I was still trying to figure out. We returned to her flat and, in separate rooms, worked on our projects into the night with a newfound enthusiasm. I began meditating, and while sitting I saw in my mind's eye image after image open doorways into my core creativity.

Being curious, willing to absorb creative stimulation and see where it leads you, can spark ideas in ways you might not expect. Attending a concert might simply be entertaining at first but then yield to a new state of absorption. You might find yourself seeing a new way of coordinating with a team of people you're working with on a project because you're observing something about the collaboration among the musicians. While it might be something obvious, sometimes it takes an experience for an idea to stick and for you to realize there's a way to apply it in your own life. Thinking about support for your own improvisations in life might spark an insight into where you are lacking a foundation for risk-taking and creativity and what you could do to change the situation.

You might also find inspiration by exploring and observing things in your everyday surroundings. John Lennon famously was inspired by the words on a circus poster on his wall to write the song "Being for the Benefit of Mr. Kite" and by a breakfast cereal commercial playing on his television to write the song "Good Morning." Many inventors have come up with ideas based on what's going on in their day-to-day lives. Steve Jobs found it annoying to have to carry around a bulky Sony Walkman and switch CDs. It inspired him to wonder how he could fit all his music on a small, sleek device that he could fit in his pocket—the seed of the idea for the Apple iPod. Wonder and curiosity can take you out of the ordinary and into the experience of a core creativity download in open mind.

RESEARCHING AND LEARNING

Exploring an art gallery, a museum, a curio shop, or going to a movie, play, or concert where you can be curious about and observe what's before you are all excellent ways to begin opening the door to the receptive state of open mind. However, you may be at the beginning of a learning curve and have a lot of research and learning to do before setting up a solid plan for your creative project or transformation. If you commit to researching and learning, if you persist, then even if you should start to doubt your abilities or become impatient, you'll strengthen your foundation for change. I've worked with people who become so exuberant about their ideas that they impulsively pursue them in a big way that involves an unnecessarily large risk, the equivalent of diving into a body of water without checking its depth first.

Research and learning isn't just for rank beginners. Many highly creative artists recognize that despite their expertise and mastery, they still have much to learn. They eagerly embrace what Buddhists call *beginner's mind*, a willingness to approach what is familiar with a fresh perspective, as if they knew nothing. They enjoy building knowledge and skills and being inspired by other artists to take new risks with their creative endeavors, so they're not afraid to find themselves at the beginning of a learning curve. In fact, they may even seek it out. George Harrison picked up a sitar on the set of the Beatles movie *Help!*, tried playing it, and committed to lessons on this difficult-to-master instrument that has three times as many strings as a guitar. His playing of the sitar on songs like "Norwegian Wood" inspired many other artists to use the instrument in their recordings, too—all because of Harrison's curiosity, exploration, and willingness to start at the beginning of a learning curve and work hard.

That level of curiosity and willingness can inspire great successes. One of my favorite examples is that of a client of mine I'll call James. A few years ago, I was counseling James, who had recently graduated from college and signed on to be an assistant to a B-movie producer, as James aspired to be a screenwriter and producer someday. His boss had turned out to be very difficult to work for and a poor mentor, leaving James very disappointed in how little he was learning. Frustrated and depressed, James saw little hope in continuing to pursue a career in film.

As I listened to him, I could see he was at the beginning of a learning curve and needed to pay his bills by sticking it out at his job, but I also recognized that he was deeply dedicated to his ultimate goal. He wasn't sure how to move forward when he had taken others' advice to get an entry-level job in the business and learn all he could, only to feel trapped.

After going over his options with me, James committed to taking some classes in psychology, which he was interested in and which he felt would help him create believable, multidimensional characters. He also recognized that what he was learning could help him not just with his writing but in interpersonal and business relationships. The action of starting classes made him feel far less helpless.

Simultaneously, James asked friends if they knew of anyone who had experience screenwriting and was willing to team up with a beginner. Through them, James found a writing partner who loved her day job but also enjoyed writing screenplays at night and on the weekends. This partner had achieved some success with writing scripts for episodic television after studying her craft with a top Los Angeles screenwriter, so there was a lot she could teach James. Writing with his partner kept him feeling connected to his goal even when he was having a particularly challenging time dealing with his boss and the boring details of his day job.

Over the next year or two, James became so driven that after work, he kept up in his psychology classes, took some screenwriting seminars and workshops, worked with his writing partner, and participated in script analysis readings for several talent agencies to better understand the elements of a good script. Then, when the screenplay was finally complete, James's more seasoned writing partner used her connections to show the screenplay to some studio executives. The next thing they knew, a studio had optioned the screenplay. In fact, they were so impressed that they asked James to produce the movie that James and his partner had written. The film was a brilliant success, and James was able to quit his day job and focus on writing and producing.

Not many people are willing to work as hard as James was at learning his craft, but his rapid success goes to show that even if it feels as if the learning curve is very steep, your willingness to do research and be a dedicated student can take you where you want to go.

If it feels as if you'll be stuck in your day job forever, you could quit and put enormous pressure on yourself, but I don't recommend it. Better to do as James did: practice patience and put yourself on a dual track, continuing to work but having a clear set of goals that will help you progress in your artistic pursuit or toward changing your career.

There are all sorts of opportunities for exploring subjects of interest. Consider taking classes through a college or university or an organization such as the New York Open Center, 1440 University, or the Esalen Institute in Big Sur. You can also take classes online, enrolling in webinars or courses such as the ones that are part of the MasterClass series. If you choose to take online classes, be honest with yourself about whether online versus in-person classes will work for you. Attending classes with like-minded people who are as engaged as you are in the subject matter can keep you motivated because you can have spontaneous conversations as you arrive in the classroom or after class ends. These types of interactions enhance the learning experience and expose you to more perspectives beyond your own or the instructor's. Teleconferencing can feel impersonal and awkward, so you might not get as much out of an online class as you would an in-person one. Also, it might feel uncomfortable to walk out of an in-person class early or skip several sessions but easy to skip an online class by logging in online but then taking yourself off-screen. When you first try online learning, be mindful and observant of its pros and cons for you.

Although research may seem like hard, boring work, explore that. Are you bored because you're forgetting the payoff to all your research?

Remember to stay on a dual track, maintaining a connection to your dream, what you want to create for yourself, even if you're still unsure of what it will look like.

DREAMWORK

As you continue doing the absorption work of exploring, observing, research, and learning, consider paying more attention to your nighttime dreams and even priming yourself to have helpful ones. Dreams are portals into open mind and can offer ideas and insights once you've interpreted them, and they can even lead to achieve breakthroughs like the ones mentioned in chapter 2, "Before You Say Hello, Say Goodbye." Breakthroughs from dreams can be big ideas—like the melody for "Yesterday" and the shape of a benzene ring were to the dreamers who dreamed them. They can also be personal insights and newfound courage or motivation. Knowing and understanding yourself better, and feeling more confident and excited about the transformation you seek, can help you persevere and heal old wounds that caused you to become insecure.

Whenever you wake up from a nightmare or a less frightening dream that you sense is important, make a point of recording it without analyzing it. Nightmares, especially recurring ones, and a strong feeling that the dream is not an ordinary one, may be the mind's way of ensuring you pay attention to intuitive wisdom bubbling up from your unconscious. Dreams can be so helpful that I suggest keeping a journal or notebook, or even your mobile phone with speech-to-text software, for recording them and cueing yourself at bedtime to remember your dreams. Silently or aloud, say to yourself a few times, "I'm going to dream a dream with an important message for me" and see what happens. Do it night after night until you get a dream that you feel you should explore afterward.

And when you awaken from a dream in the morning or in the middle of the night, don't stop to analyze it or connect it to something you experienced in your everyday life. Focus on recording it, every detail that you can remember. Keeping your eyes closed while you do this can help.

When you're ready to analyze the dream, pay attention to any connections to your everyday experiences that could shed some light on the meaning. Identify any emotions you had in the dream in response to what unfolded. As you try to make sense of the symbols and people or animals in your dream, keep in mind that according to gestalt therapy, each represents some aspect of yourself. Imagine inhabiting that unicycle or snow-capped mountain, or what the faceless figure urging you to follow it into a house would say to you. Fritz Perls, the founder of gestalt therapy, taught that you should ask the client who is sharing details of a dream, "What's missing?" By thinking about what is missing, you start a valuable inquiry you might not have otherwise engaged in.

I had a dream in 1989 or 1990 that gave me insight and courage: In it, I was walking through Central Park at night by myself when I was suddenly approached by three men who were going to attack me. I became enraged and suddenly realized I was wearing a backpack in which there was a fold-up umbrella I could use as a weapon. In my dream, I had time to remove my backpack, take it out, and wield it against my attackers, pummeling them and driving them off. The dream was so intense and vivid that I woke up in a sweat and immediately wrote it down, sensing that it bore an important message for me.

The next morning, I recorded all that I could remember, and then I analyzed it. Fritz Perls's question came to mind: What was missing? *A weapon in the front of my body.* All I had was that umbrella-containing backpack on my back. Then I used a gestalt dream interpretation technique and played the role of the backpack, which told me, "I'm like a student's backpack. You have resources here—textbooks, your lunch, snacks, keys to get into your house, money, an umbrella, and so on." The message was that while I might not think I have resources to draw on in a dangerous situation, while they might not appear in front of me or in the forefront of my mind, they're present for me.

Using a Gestalt Inquiry Technique to let the symbols inform me of their meaning (a technique I'll explain shortly), I next learned what the small, fold-up umbrella represented. It said, "I'm protective. I'm a weapon. If you use me, you can do serious harm. You're not helpless because I'm right here in your backpack." Then, my mind flashed back to a real-life experience that bore a strong resemblance to the dream. Six months or so before, in the summer, when the Central Park jogger attack was in the news each night, I'd had dinner with some people on the Upper West Side of Manhattan, and afterward one of them asked me to accompany one of the dinner guests home. The woman lived on the Upper East Side and was understandably nervous about her plan to walk alone across Central Park. I was doing a lot of running in those days and had my running shoes on, and while I could have said, "Sure, I'll accompany her—I'll call a cab"—for whatever reason, I readily agreed to walk with her. We got to her apartment safely, but when I was crossing back to the Upper West Side, where I lived, I saw about a half dozen teenagers, one of whom was holding what appeared to be a hunting knife while another clearly had a handgun tucked into his pants. I tore off as quickly as I could and, fortunately, outran them.

At the time, I thought that since I'd escaped the danger, there was no reason to think about the frightening event any further. My nightmare months later told me that I had not completely processed my fear or gleaned the message from the experience. My unconscious was giving me another chance to learn the lesson and let go of my fear, so I took it.

GESTALT INQUIRY TECHNIQUE

Gestalt, from a German word meaning "whole" and developed by Frederic Perls and his wife, Laura, is an approach to accessing what's in the unconscious so that it can be combined with what the conscious mind knows, forming a more holistic view of what you're experiencing. Gestalt integrates mind and body and is a here-and-now therapeutic approach, helping you better understand your issues and challenges of today rather than focusing on your past and the origins of your problems (which is the aim of analytic therapies). Using gestalt techniques can give you powerful insights into what your unconscious knows and feels that is hidden from your everyday awareness.

A common gestalt technique is to imagine inhabiting objects, figures, or selves speaking to you. After my nightmare about being mugged in Central Park, I learned more about my unconscious wisdom by taking a few minutes to meditate so I could enter the transformative state of open mind and then inhabit the backpack from my dream, then the knife, and then the running shoes to learn what they could teach me. You, too, can do this with objects or figures in your dream. When you are in a state of open mind, ask a question of the object or figure and then take a few moments to feel that you are not you, the questioner, but the object or figure. Then answer the question. When you get your answer, you can switch back to being present within yourself, the person interested in your unconscious wisdom, and ask another question, continuing this switching off as long as necessary to get the insights you're seeking.

You can use this technique to question your "selves" too—for example, your "head" or logical self, your "heart" or core feeling self, and your "wisdom" or wise inner self. Allow yourself plenty of time to role play with the various voices inside of yourself that represent aspects of you. If you're wrestling with a challenge, such as what you want to do about a conflict you're having in a relationship or a loss of passion in your creative work, you can start with embodying your logical self and speaking about your ideas and thoughts. You could even write down what your logical self has to say. Next, embody your feeling self and let your heart speak—aloud or on paper. Then, embody your wisdom self to learn what it has to say. After that, you could embody any ideas or thoughts that came to you—the idea of taking a break from a relationship, for example, or finding a collaborative partner to help you with your problematic creative project. Let this thought share more ideas and feelings with you.

Erving Polster, a renowned gestalt therapist, says that there are a multiplicity of selves always present and operating, especially around any decision you're facing. Embodying various "selves" to connect with what they know moves them from being disparate to working together, giving you a more holistic view of anything you're struggling with. Some believe that everything in a dream—objects, other people, energetic forces such as a storm—represents an aspect of yourself, so it makes sense to use a gestalt technique to help you understand what a dream is trying to tell you.

Most dreams offer clues to what's unfinished or unexpressed in our lives. Working with them can help you complete unfinished business. I thought about that night in New York City and how I hadn't checked in with myself about how comfortable I was being this other person's protector when I was unarmed. I thought about how in fact I'd had four very important resources: my ability to run very fast for a long time, my running shoes on my feet, my mindfulness that caused me to observe that the teenagers had weapons and were dangerous, and my quick thinking. I further realized that the umbrella and the anger I used wielding it represented my anger at myself for not practicing self-care. I could have been mindful of my anxiousness about walking through Central Park and instead of going along with the suggestion to walk the other dinner guest across the park, offer to hail a cab, but I was ignoring my feelings.

Thanks to the dream, I experienced a shift as the old fear I'd had left over from that frightening experience in Central Park finally lifted. I became more committed to putting my need to look out for my well-being ahead of my need to satisfy other people's requests. And I felt more confident in my ability to take care of myself should unexpected danger appear—and when I'm feeling pressured to take risks I don't want to take.

My assistant, Rhonda Bryant, had a recurring disturbing dream since childhood. In it, an animal or person was trying to kill her, and she was scared she wouldn't be able to get away, so she would curl up, become still, and play dead—and then she would wake up. Recurring dreams can have somewhat different details each time, but the similarities are many and worth noting. In adulthood, Rhonda says, "When I read about Bessel van der Kolk's work that found that trauma patients don't feel safe in their bodies and how yoga can help, I had an epiphany: I was sexually molested at a very young age and as a child repressed all the memories and feelings of this trauma. But I couldn't suppress my dreams." Rhonda recognized that when she was a little girl, she would pretend to be curled up and asleep in order to survive the molestation psychologically. While she was undergoing therapy and energy work (reiki, for example) to clear old traumas, she was finding that she continued to be easily triggered into dissociation—a state in which she mentally checked out of the situation she was in.

To further clear the old trauma, Rhonda decided to try lucid dreaming, in which a part of you is aware during the dream, allowing you to orchestrate how it unfolds. She went to sleep at night determined to have a helpful dream—maybe the recurring nightmare—but also, to experience within it her power to change what was happening. When she dreamed of a pack of wild dogs chasing her, she became aware that she had choices within the dream and responded this way:

Instead of playing dead, I felt this powerful energy force flow through my body, which I directed at the charging dogs through my eyes, and I commanded them to sit. To my amazement, the dogs stopped. I knew the energy force was only temporary, so I started to look for a place to be safe. A woman was walking in the other direction, and I told her about the dogs. She said we could go to her home, so we started walking in that direction. Every so often I would turn around and focus the energy at the dogs to keep them at bay. We finally made it to her home and locked the door to keep them out. Then out of the blue the woman said, "You should take the Nia White Belt Training." Talk about a validation that I was on the right track—I had been considering taking this class that promised to help me feel safe and comfortable in my body. I did—and it was very helpful. Of course, achieving that goal of feeling safe from physical and sexual abuse and trauma is an ongoing process, and I know it's important to continue the dialogue with my body. But now whenever I feel threatened, I tap into the power I accessed in my dream to help keep me grounded and centered.[11]

I've worked with people whose dreams gave them a powerful message about what to do as well as the motivation to do it—start a new project, leave behind a career, and so on. Don't overlook the tool of dreamwork in your quest to achieve open mind and get a download of intuitive wisdom, strength, and ideas.

CONNECT WITH NATURE

When I want to go into a state of open mind, I'll often connect with nature, swimming for twenty minutes in a lake or ocean. I often get inspiration and can see in my mind's eye entire chapters of my writing. My father modeled to me that even after a long workday or work week in an office, it's important to leave behind brick and mortar, cement and asphalt, artificial lights and sounds, and city life to be among the trees and birds. He was a member of the Thoreau Society and regularly took time to walk in the woods near where we lived.

The advice to take a long walk in a forest to clear your head and receive inspiration is rooted in the fact that in nature, we effortlessly shift into a different mind state. Our levels of the stress hormone cortisol drop in as little as ten to fifteen minutes.[12] A 2015 Stanford University study found that walking in nature reduces activity in the area of the brain associated with rumination, that is, overthinking that can cause feelings of anxiety.[13]

In nature, your parasympathetic nervous system switches on, relaxing you. According to Kaplan's attention restoration theory, in nature, you don't feel your focus pulled in a certain direction or feel you must stop and analyze stimulation, so you're better able to focus on what you feel is important to you. According to the research done for the book *Daily Rituals: How Artists Work* (2013), a large percentage of artists take a daily walk in nature as a ritual for accessing their creativity.[14] Steve Jobs, who created Apple computers and served as Apple's CEO for years, was famous for taking walks in nature whenever he wanted to imagine or contemplate a design concept or make a tough business decision.

A long walk or bike ride out in nature can not only feel restorative but shift you into open mind, whether or not you experience curiosity and no-self on the way to that mind state. Actor Cody Fern says he makes a point of getting out in nature, which for him is "returning to source . . . the mountains and the forests are the most healing. They revive my spirits and wash clean my thoughts. There is nothing like a five-day hike through the true wilderness, you and the elements and the burning questions."[15] Like many artists, Taylor Swift chose to use her time during the pandemic to create art—and she reconnected with nature, too, which helped inspire songs like "Seven" found on her sister albums, *Folklore* and *Evermore*.[16] She was onto something: performance on creative, problem-solving tasks improved 50 percent for fifty-six women who unplugged, leaving behind cell phones and tablets to spend four days hiking in nature, according to a 2012 study.[17]

WHERE DO IDEAS ULTIMATELY ORIGINATE?

Whether you sit quietly, walk meditatively, or take other actions that allow you to absorb stimulation from your unconscious or from the world around you, you are likely to slip into open mind at some point. From there, you recognize that you have access to ideas that were hidden from you when you're in an ordinary waking state. Some say that you're not just drawing in ideas and insights from what's in your personal unconscious but from something larger—even a spiritual source perhaps. For example, the ancient Greeks believed that creative ideas came from nine goddesses who bestowed inspiration on humans.

I've always been fascinated by how creative artists describe their process. Inevitably, they talk about being in a state of open mind where the download of core creativity can happen, even though they use their own words to explain this experience. James Taylor said in a 2015 *Hemispheres* magazine interview, "Given enough empty time, the songs show up. I've often said that it's an unconscious and mysterious process, my type of songwriting. You really are just waiting to hear it, and you have to be in a place where you can receive the song, more than generate it. There's just something about songwriting. It's like a musical puzzle or a math problem. When you solve it, it's like you're being surprised by your own subconscious in a way. That's an unparalleled delight."[18] Robbie Robertson of the Band said in the documentary *Once Were Brothers*, "The creative process is a process catching you off guard. You write about what you know, where you have been, who you knew and know. . . . Creativity comes from the womb of emptiness."[19]

In 2016, Bruce Springsteen told *Rolling Stone* magazine,

You're always in a box, and you're an escape artist if you do what I do—or if you're a creative person, period. You build your box and then you escape from it. You build another one and you escape from it. That's ongoing. And you may at some point escape enough boxes where you find yourself back around to the first one again and you go, "Oh, I didn't think I had any more to say about these things. Wait a minute, yes, I do. I've got a lot more to say about these things!"[20]

And in a 2020 interview for *AARP: The Magazine*, Bruce Springsteen said,

You have your antenna out. You're just walking through the world and you're picking up these signals of emotions and spirit and history and events, today's events and past remembrances. These things you divine from the air are all intangible elements: spirit, emotion, history. These are the tools of the songwriter's trade before he even picks up the pen. . . . People who are attuned to that atmosphere usually end up being artists of some sort. If you are attuned you pick up on the information and with the desire to record, you learn a language to do so whether it's paintings, films, songs or poetry.[21]

Helen Mirren said in an interview with Robert Love for *AARP: The Magazine*, "I would say there is a spirituality in being a human being that is connected to the imagination in some way. . . . I find the engagement in the imagination very appealing." Love points out that in her autobiography, Mirren wrote, "The theatre became my religion, and I wanted to serve it."[22] And songwriter Leonard Cohen summed up absorption and surrender to open mind in his song "A Thousand Kisses Deep," written with Sharon Robinson, where he says, "You lose your grip and then you slip into the masterpiece."[23]

What are you surrendering to when you experience a downflow of core creativity? Painter Ronnie Landfield says, "My work comes from my connection to the universe."[24] Actor Jodi Long says, "Whether I am singing, dancing, playing an instrument, or acting, I am just channeling the Universal energy through me."[25]

Many people believe that ideas can come from what Carl Jung called the collective unconscious—which all human beings share. It's here that the archetypes of stories, themes, and characters are said to reside, seeping into our conscious and unconscious and influencing our perceptions about ourselves and our lives. You can tap into your personal unconscious, but some would say that you can also access what's in the collective unconscious, too.

You might believe that ideas are coming only from your own unconscious mind, but in my many years of working with creative people, I've found that curiosity about the ultimate origin of the ideas and insights that come to us, as well as the power of core creativity and intuition, can lead to explorations about one's spiritual nature. That can result in valuable discoveries and help people find a sense of purpose, optimism, and comfort. It's a payoff you might not be aware of as you use the ideas in this book to expand your creativity to help you with transformation and bringing your dreams to fruition, but it's one I hope you'll keep in mind as you read more about open mind and what it offers you.

Stillness, exploring, observing, researching, learning, and working with dreams and intuition are all essential components of taking in stimulation and ideas that can help you, but then you have to take action and work with the ideas that come to you or generate ideas through rituals of action. Even after Paul McCartney dreamed the entire melody for "Yesterday," he had to come up with lyrics and an arrangement. While inspiring ideas and insights may have come to you as a result of tapping into your core creativity and intuition, you have more work to do to turn those ideas into something bigger, building on them as you continue to tap into your core creativity again and again.

Chapter Six

Generating Ideas and Other Ways into Open Mind

Generating ideas complements the many ways of absorbing them. You might be crafting an idea that came to you when you were absorbing, or you might simply "noodle" or "play around"—take action that you're not certain will be productive—until a fresh idea comes to you. Musicians I've worked with have often said they'll pick up an instrument and begin playing without a specific goal in mind. What emerges might not be all that interesting or impressive, but it can soon give way to an idea that's worth building on. Many creative artists will even noodle at a secondary art—painting or sculpture, for example—to get into a state of open mind that can lead to breakthroughs in their primary art or even in their self-awareness. What looks like unproductive noodling might actually be a ritual that the artist knows will take them into a state of open mind. However, they have to trust in the process of generating ideas—noodling and the ritual of regularly working at their craft. Often, the challenge is to silence the inner critic, the one that says, "You're wasting time."

THE INNER CRITIC

If you're like a lot of people, your ego, a voice within that is highly critical, will interfere with you as you're generating ideas. You have to quiet that fearful inner critic that's trying to stop you with thoughts like "This is impractical" or "I don't have what it takes" or "You're making a fool of yourself" by allowing yourself to become curious and available to be inspired. Grammy Award-winning music producer Val Garay says, "You've got to trust your instincts and don't second guess yourself—that's the death move."[1] Painter Ronnie Landfield said that as a child, "I knew that I was not Superman, and I could not fly but the main archetypes for me were heroes who always trusted themselves."[2] Trust yourself, and trust in the creative process as you continue to absorb creative stimulation and ideas and work with them, generating new ideas to add on to them.

When preparing to play Jerry Lee Lewis in the movie *Great Balls of Fire* (1989), award-winning actor Dennis Quaid, who is also a musician and songwriter leading a band called the Sharks, says, "I had Jerry Lee over my shoulder, saying you're doing it wrong, Son. You're doing it wrong the entire time. . . . You always have that voice that's in your ear whether it's from an external source or your own telling you 'You probably suck.' But you have to banish that voice and not listen to it!"[3] Actor Jodi Long says, "It's important not to yield in a destructive way to the negative voice that may be gnawing at you in our head. Just note it and say, I need to take a break."[4] Breaks can shut down your ego's fears. Meditating to explore those fears and bring them into your conscious mind can help you release them. Be sure to go back to chapter 2, "Before You Say Hello, Say Good-bye" and do some of the meditations offered there—and try the No-Self Way to Core Creativity Meditation, which you'll find later in this chapter.

One way the inner critic can impede your progress is by causing you to become stuck in the role of student. There are actors who take class after class but don't go on auditions, and writers who have reams of material but who have never ventured to submit their writing anywhere. As with absorbing by doing research and exposing yourself to stimulation, when you're generating ideas, you can become stuck in the activity, unaware that you're spinning your wheels.

I once had a client who was writing a novel and dutifully showed up at the same coffee shop daily to work on her writing. After two years, she was frustrated that she didn't have a completed manuscript. I told her to bring in her rough draft so we could look at it together. Right away, I could see the problem: she was jumping around and jotting down ideas and words but not editing, expanding on, or crafting anything she had written. I suggested she work with a novel-writing coach to set up a schedule for her process so that every day she knew exactly what she was working on and hoped to finish writing. You might need to hire someone to help you set up a schedule and process for completing your project, particularly if you have ADHD or other issues that make it difficult for you to get organized. And, remember, a Creativity Support Pod can hold you accountable for sticking to that schedule.

If you're certain you don't want to take the next natural step with your work and do it professionally or share it with an audience but you enjoy engaging in your art, there's no reason you have to leave your practice room. But are you sure that's what you want to do? Are you sure that you don't want to expand upon what you're doing, set goals, and complete a project? Your inner critic might be telling you that changing how you spend your time is unrealistic or that you'll fail if you try to "go big." Do you want that voice to prevail?

Another way to quiet your inner critic is to use the energy of fear to fuel you as you move forward into taking action. Dennis Quaid's strategy is to "just take that fear and squeeze it and use it instead of trying to avoid it or talking [yourself] out of it. Just use it because the fear is energy—and you can actually use it to your own advantage if you can control it." He also says he will place that fear between his stomach and his spine: "It makes you very focused . . . then it will just fall away."[5]

Because I had often experienced a sympathetic nervous system response before doing workshops, I asked my friend and mentor, spiritual teacher and author Ram Dass, "Aren't you frightened when you talk in front of a group of a thousand people? It scares the hell out of me when I'm about to talk to just one hundred." He told me that, yes, he would get nervous—his heart would beat quickly, his thoughts would race, and his hands would turn sweaty. He would tune in to those physical symptoms and use the energy of nervousness as an "inner engine" to fuel an excellent talk. He would sometimes tell the audience, "It's Ram Dass, and he's not supposed to be nervous, but he is"—and everyone would laugh. That shifted him out of intense nervousness and made it easier for him to begin speaking.[6]

You might find that using the Body Observation Meditation you learned about earlier helps you release fear or rechannel it. And if you've done meditations in which you've anchored the energy of courage in your body, meditate and draw on that stored energy.

In *Buddha's Little Instruction Book* (1994), author Jack Kornfield wrote, "The heart is like a garden. It can grow compassion or fear, resentment or love. What seeds will you plant there?"[7] With practice at expressing your creativity, you'll find it easier to avoid harsh, negative self-judgments and cultivate self-compassion, which will support you in your creative endeavors. You can also use the following Mindful Self-Compassion Visualization.

MINDFUL SELF-COMPASSION VISUALIZATION

Sit comfortably, paying attention to the rhythm and flow of your breathing. Then, bring your focus and attention to the area above and between your eyebrows as well as to your heart. Take three long, slow breaths in and out, and on the last out breath, bring your focus to feeling a deep and abiding sense of love and compassion.

Now visualize in your mind's eye that you are connected to a glowing ball of golden light that is the deep resource of love and compassion. Direct this golden ball of light filled with love and compassion to move to the top of your head, where it radiates golden rays downward through your entire body. Feel your heart filling with the love and compassion that flows from the rays of this light. Remain present with the experience of being infused with love, kindness, and compassion.

Repeat softly to yourself:

I wish you to be free of suffering.
I wish you to experience love and compassion.
I wish you to be happy.
I wish you to be free of suffering.
I wish you to become filled and infused with abiding love and loving compassion.

See and hear yourself connecting with the deep resource of love, kindness, and compassion. Notice how you feel in your heart space. Pay attention to the quality of warmth and flowing energy of compassion, kindness, and love flowing through you, healing any pain or suffering and opening you up into a space of happiness. Then, quietly say the following:

May I become free of suffering.
May I experience all pain leaving.

May I experience love, compassion, and kindness.
May I become free of suffering.

Continue to notice the qualities of energy filling your heart space as you experience love, compassion, and kindness until you are ready to end the visualization.

Also, you may have to accept that you might have to be willing to generate something awful before you create something good. Eagles singer, songwriter, and guitarist Glenn Frey says that early in his career, singer-songwriter Bob Seger was mentoring him and told him that if he wanted to hit it big, he had to write his own songs. "Well, what if they're bad?" Frey asked. Seger replied that he should keep writing until eventually he wrote a good song.[8]

A "good enough for now and getting better" mind-set—that is, a growth mind-set—can help you silence the inner critic. As you develop more self-awareness (and, remember, mindfulness practice develops the self-awareness center of the brain), you'll find it easier to acknowledge and explore your qualities and habits without harsh negative self-judgments, becoming not a harsh critic but a helpful one as you admit that you might need more practice in some area. You'll see you can change your habits and relate to your qualities differently as you come to see their pros, cons, and neutrality in different situations. Being a perfectionist can be good, bad, or neutral, but if your perfectionism takes the form of a harsh inner critic continually berating you, continue your mindfulness practice to quiet that voice. Otherwise, your inner critic will prevent playful experimenting that can lead to creative breakthroughs.

Of course, sometimes your inner critic will have some insights worth listening to. Maybe you would benefit from being more prepared before setting out on a new journey. More practice and a greater stockpile of resources could be very helpful. If you quell the fear your inner critic whips up inside you, it will be easier to listen to both your rational mind and your intuition as it sends you messages. Most often, however, the inner critic is simply the voice of old fears, and it has nothing important to reveal to you. Open mind can help you access your intuitive wisdom, which can guide you around obstacles.

I know someone I'll call Fran, a prolific writer of articles and books who had been working for some time on a screenplay, became stuck but had a breakthrough once she went into a state of open mind: Fran realized that for this particular project, she wanted to write it as a novel and would consider rewriting the screenplay after that. She immediately began converting what she had written into a narrative and felt herself in creative flow. She realized that her ego had been attached to writing the story as a screenplay because she had written a complete screenplay before and it had achieved some accolades even though it had never been made into a movie. She had felt confident and enthusiastic about writing a new script about a different story, but soon after beginning the writing, she started to hear and read that writers like her who are skilled at writing novels shouldn't bother trying to write screenplays because they can't make the leap to the new form.

Not realizing she was internalizing these messages that she consciously had rejected, Fran kept plugging away at the work. When her intuition was telling her there was a reason this new screenplay was much harder for her to write than the last one had been, her ego got in the way and kept her struggling with the script when she was no longer enjoying the work or feeling as optimistic as she had before. It took an "aha!" moment of insight in a state of open mind for her to acknowledge what she knew deep down: she really wanted to switch forms.

The time she spent in generating and shaping the screenplay wasn't wasted, however, because she was working on some of the elements that go into a novel, such as character development, dialogue, and plot. But she recognized she wasted a lot of time feeling frustrated because she wanted to prove to her inner critic that she could write a second screenplay. Realizing that, she went with her instinct to make the writing easier and more enjoyable by converting the screenplay to a novel.

Years ago, when I met Michael Crichton while both of us were teaching at UCLA, he said he had been told that he couldn't write for Hollywood because he was "just an MD." Fortunately, he ignored that pronouncement. Don't feel you have to "stick to your lane" even if people criticize you. Bob Dylan was booed when performing at the Newport Pop Festival because he dared to play an electric guitar while dressed in black leather as he sang "Ain't Going to Work on Maggie's Farm No More," an anthem he'd penned to demarcate his creative leap in his and the culture's music. The audience had been expecting him to strum an acoustic guitar while playing and singing a folk song, and they didn't take well to the unexpected change. Bob Dylan did just fine after making that bold choice, and many albums later, he now paints, sculpts, and welds, expressing himself creatively through forms that some might say "aren't his lane." He's a testament to the importance of listening to your instincts. (And speaking of Dylan, both George Harrison and John Lennon said that Dylan taught them to consider integrating their personal feelings and experiences into their songwriting—advice they took that led them to dare to change the songwriting formulas that had served them well to that point in the Beatles' career.)

Listening to your instincts and being true to what feels right to you can be hard when you're worried about how others might respond. You might want to take out a journal and write about any stifling messages you've received regarding what types of generating activities you "should" be doing. What "should" are you holding onto? Whose voice do you hear when you identify a "should" statement? Where did it originate? Think about going back to chapter 3, "Reclaim Your Creative Self," and working with the Return to the Scene to Change It Visualization so that the message implanted in your unconscious is one you've consciously chosen and that supports your changing lanes and exploring new ways of expressing yourself.

The act of generating ideas can involve noodling, brainstorming, or playing around with ideas, often with other people who can contribute to an improvisational conversation. These activities can shift you into open mind. Here's how Dennis Quaid described refining or crafting your way into experiencing open mind, core creativity, and your intuition: "You learn to craft, and you learn the technique to the point where you're not even aware that you're using the technique anymore. It just becomes a part of you. And that's the jumping off point into art. Art can come, but art needs to be directed and molded." Dennis also shared that when he's not acting, he's either in the studio writing or heading out on the road with his band the Sharks, because it inspires him, gets him more deeply in touch, and makes him feel "really alive."[9]

If listening to your gut earns you resistance from others involved in your efforts, consider whether the pushback is coming from someone who is envious of your ability to slow down and not be working 24/7. Is the voice telling you to give up coming from someone who wishes they had the courage to take creative risks like you do? Is their advice valuable to some degree but, like so many messages from ego, rooted in fear that was born from their past experiences? But keep in mind that if you're looking to take a big creative risk, such as opening your own restaurant or starting a new career in midlife, resistance from others can inspire you to do more research and better set yourself up for success than if you completely ignored the words of a naysayer. Your gut may be right after all—your dream might turn out to be all that you had hoped it would be—but take the middle road. Don't overreact or underreact to others' questioning of that big "yes" you received intuitively when you meditated with the intention of gaining insights about your project.

As you become more self-aware and get more practice going into open mind, accessing core creativity and your intuition, you will find it easier to go with your gut even when it means standing up to the crowd or even to your closest supporters. You'll trust yourself and hold firm to your creative choices.

ABSORBING AND GENERATING AND BACK AGAIN

If you've been generating ideas for a while and are dissatisfied, you might feel overwhelmed or frustrated. You might not be spending enough time in absorption and stillness. Actor Cody Fern says, "Balance is a difficult thing for me to strike—and the shakeup usually comes from an external source, exhaustion or a breakdown. . . . Ironically, the breakdown often leads to the breakthrough. I'm working more in my life now to be kinder to myself and trust and allow that the breakthrough will come without grinding myself into the ground."[10]

If you're resistant to stepping out of the activity of generating, remember that being still, in a state of absorption, *is* "doing something" toward your goal of creating something new for yourself. Painter Ronnie Landfield also says, "Pay attention to your inner voice and you will know when to stop, and if you listen or when you listen then change will come. I teach and tell all of my students that you are not the same every day; you need to tune in and to listen to your inner voice."[11] Could it be telling you to stop, listen, and observe?

Do you tend to procrastinate and distract yourself? Keep in mind Amy Ziering's beliefs about creativity and the creative process: "Count on the hard work, bank on that, figure out what interests you and you want to get up every day and do, and then work at it, don't wait for inspiration. Just work at it, even if it's boring, even if you don't want to do it, even if you don't understand; and in that, at least for me, creativity finds you, and you find it."[12] You can find a balance between activity, stillness, and absorbing. Creative artists I've talked to find the shifting process from one brain network to another natural and intuitive. That may be due to practice at experiencing brain functional connectivity, a phenomenon I mentioned in chapter 1, "The Deepest Creativity Comes from Your Core." The stronger the interconnectivity among several brain regions, the greater a person's ability to experience divergent thinking, develop fresh images in the visual arts, improvise musically, and use language figuratively. In other words, it's not that one area of the brain is richer in neural connections than another but that the very creative person is using several areas of the brain collaboratively. They're receiving input, crafting it, and effortlessly shaping it into something novel as they experience the flow of core creativity. Multiple sections of their brain are lit up with activity.

According to research, the systems of the brain that communicate with each other effectively, sharing neural networks for exchanging information, have been identified as the *default mode network*, the *executive control network*, and the *salience network*. We're using our default mode network when we're engaged in imagination or simply letting our mind wander—and this network is active when we're retrieving memories. When we use our executive network, we're making decisions and problem solving. The salience network is our inner editor: we use it when we decide what we'll take note of and what we'll ignore. In other words, we need these three networks to function well and communicate with each other through neural networks so that we can shift among daydreaming, analyzing our ideas, and discerning what is and isn't important to explore further.

It makes sense that people who have weaker interconnectivity among these regions would get stuck overthinking things or imagining but not being able to build on the ideas that come to them when their minds have done some exploring. While you might not be looking to write a hit song or choreograph a Broadway show, you can build the interconnections among these three networks so you can more easily solve problems related to your career, relationships, or life goals and break

through any obstacles that seem to be holding you back. I have observed
that shifting from absorbing stimulation to daydreaming to generating
ideas and crafting them becomes much easier with practice.[13]

The creativity process is not linear or sequential. It's organic. You
move among the three networks of your brain, intuitively deciding what
to do next. And you let go, tune in, and move forward: You let go of
the grip of your ego and its fear, biases, and limitations. You tune in
to core creativity by achieving an open mind state, however you get to
that state. You move forward into taking action as a result of receiving
ideas or insights.

Intuition, which you access through mindfulness practice, guides you
in deciding when to stop gathering information and being stimulated by
all that's out there and when to start processing it, or to start crafting,
or to go from crafting to "not doing" and then to stimulation and so on.

If you get frustrated with generating ideas or engaging in an editing
and shaping process and feel you're hammering away yet making no
progress, you might suddenly find yourself in open mind experiencing
creative flow. But you can also take a break and shift into absorbing,
taking a walk in the woods, watching a film, sitting in a garden, or reading a book. Listen to your gut about whether to continue or shift into
absorption.

NO-SELF AS A HALLWAY INTO OPEN MIND

If despite using the methods of absorbing, generating, and going back
and forth between them to enter open mind, you find yourself resistant,
try addressing the common obstacle of the egoic mind and embracing
what Buddhists call a state of "no-self."

Your ego and its fears that cause it to be a harsh inner critic—along
with its attachments to who you are, who you would like to become,
and the form your project or transformation will take—might generate
resistance to creative downloads. To get back into the creative flow, you
must be willing to be open to new ways of thinking and perceiving—
even if you feel you know a lot about a topic or feel your self-image and
your plans do not need adjusting. You want to be able to see the familiar
as if it were new, which requires letting go of your biases—conscious
or unconscious—and cynicism. If you're presented with a wildly dif-

ferent way of looking at your situation or achieving your goals, would you resist that perspective? For example, it's common to see yourself as a victim and others as persecutors holding you back. It can feel much more comfortable to focus on other people's roles in your difficulties than to look at your own. Be willing to become a beginner, lacking cynicism and full of curiosity about what you can do differently. Be willing to drop into a state of no-self, in which your ego—your sense of individuality—falls away. The ego is driven by fear, and its perceptions have been shaped by past experiences. Your goal is to reduce its loud voice to a mere whisper at best so that new possibilities can enter your consciousness.

Ironically, having greater self-awareness can make it easier to drop into a state of no-self. Trouble dropping into no-self can indicate that you need to do more meditation practice and more work to let go of the fears that cause you to resist change and cling to the known (including what you know about yourself). You might have abilities you've yet to discover. Being willing to let go of your limited ideas about who you are and what you can do will open your eyes to hidden potential so you can claim it.

Being in no-self allows you to enter the stillness of a void that you soon realize is not empty but quite fertile with ideas and possibilities. This "void" will soon reveal to you that it's an open field of energy. Here, it feels as if insects and birds are communicating, radio waves and cell phone signals are going out, and seedlings are pushing through the soil to the sun. In this receptive state, it's as if you're opening a zip file and eagerly experiencing an automatic download. You might need to be patient as the download begins. You might not get a big "aha!" right away, but you're very likely to get some clarity or inspiration as you remain in a receptive and curious state, flexible about what you'll experience as ideas bubble up from deep within like a geyser, bringing forth a wellspring of rich, creative imagery and thoughts.

Allow. Surrender. Both core creativity and intuitive wisdom and knowledge can be accessed in open mind not because you *have* an open mind, or are *trying* to be open minded, but because you are in a state of pure receptivity that evolves naturally after you have experienced the emptiness you have given yourself over to. Try the No-Self Way to Core Creativity Meditation to see if it helps you drop your ego and enter open mind.

NO-SELF WAY TO CORE CREATIVITY MEDITATION

Set the intention to let go of your ego and become curious, receptive, and willing to discover something new. Remember that as you enter no-self, you will be letting go of some preconceived notions such as who you are, what you can do, and what possibilities are available to you. You will feel all these notions drop away, freeing you to experience open mind and access core creativity.

Begin your meditation. Allow yourself to become receptive to something beyond the distracting chatter of your generating mind. You want to be in a state of absorbing mind and receptivity, noticing what you are experiencing but not generating thoughts. If they do arise, let them float away like clouds. After your string of distracting thoughts has slowed down or even stopped, remain present in a feeling of receptivity and absorption for at least a minute or two.

Then, allow yourself to experience "no-self." Here, your identity drops away as you simply experience being present in this experience. Let yourself disappear, allowing all fixed and limited notions of who you are or how your creative project should unfold to fall away. What I'm describing is like what you do during mindfulness meditation, where thoughts and feelings arise, exist, and fade away without your intervening to hold onto them. When this occurs, you will find yourself not in ego mind fixated upon what you think you know but instead feeling curious and open to receiving and discovering.

Recognize that now you have entered a void, a pristine emptiness. Remain here even if it's somewhat uncomfortable because you'll soon notice that this void is actually a fertile one, revealing itself to be filled with ideas, images, pictures, colors, textures, stillness, and possibility. Now experience that potential before you, all around you, and within you. Allow yourself to absorb or take in whatever you need, letting it download into you, knowing you can work with this energy of possibility to make it manifest into form. As you do so, you are downloading core creativity. Be fully present in this experience, observing it, noting what you are feeling, understanding, hearing, and seeing in your mind's eye.

When you are ready, end the meditation.

After doing the No-Self Way to Core Creativity Meditation, you might want to write in your journal about your experience of curiosity, receptivity, and the "clear the desk" experience of no-self. Pay attention to whether it is unsettling—and, if so, whether it is unsettling in a good way, a bad way, or a neutral way. You might be surprised by how the temporary discomfort of losing your sense of self wasn't so bad after all and led you into open mind and then the fertile void of ideas even as you felt the power of your core creativity and intuitive abilities at hand. Record any impressions and ideas or insights that came to you.

Now that you have discovered entryways into open mind where you can access core creativity and intuition, the work of creativity can continue as you develop habits that will support you—the subject we'll turn to next.

Chapter Seven

Mind-sets and Habits
of Highly Creative People

As you continue using portals to open mind so you can access core creativity and intuition as well as build your confidence in your creative abilities, you'll also want to start adopting some of the mind-sets and habits of highly creative people. Then it will be easier for you to tap into core creativity and use it for whatever you would like to create or change.

The mind-sets and habits I'm sharing here might feel unnatural to you at first, but I have seen how they work for people, allowing them to live more adventurously and experience remarkable transformations. As you read, I hope you'll remain open minded about new ways of thinking and operating.

BE SOLUTIONS ORIENTED
AS YOU CREATE A VISION FOR YOURSELF

For many people, the default is to focus on problems. A solutions orientation means focusing on what you would like to create and experience, crafting a vision that can inspire you even when challenges and obstacles threaten to demoralize you. What would it look like if all your problems were already solved and you felt happy and fulfilled as you expressed yourself without feeling constricted or judged? If you no longer had money challenges, if you had people around you who encouraged you, if you had already figured out how to overcome any roadblocks to living a life of purpose, fulfillment, and creativity, what would that look like?

You might want to use chapter 3's Day in the Future Visualization more than once to help you form and further develop your vision. Listen to your intuition and tap into your core creativity for ideas on what you might create. Then, you'll need to do some research into how to get from where you are to where you want to be. Having a vision that inspires you can make it easier to tackle any problems you're facing currently or that come up as you're in transition.

As you do your research, investigate how others have achieved the goals you're creating for yourself. If they had resources you didn't have, how could you acquire them? Bring your challenges to your Wisdom Council of Support and Creativity Support Pod members to see what ideas, insights, and resources they can offer you.

You might want to construct a vision board to feel an emotional connection to what you want to experience. You can do this using computer software or a poster—some people like to use three-part cardboard display posters that can be purchased at an office supply store. Fasten to your vision board words, photographs, and printed images representing aspects of your vision: what you want to do, achieve, or experience. At first, you might not know what you want written or depicted there. Google "vision boards" to get ideas. To work with the board, meditate for a minute before gazing at it. Take mindful pauses to gaze at the images; they will remind you of what you're trying to bring into manifestation.

Make working with your vision board a ritual of absorption and allowing as you let yourself shift into a state of open mind. Try to feel an emotional connection to what you're seeing. You can also glance at your vision board casually in the hopes of feeling a jolt of inspiration, but I recommend giving yourself time to feel a connection to what you've illustrated or written. You might also incorporate into your ritual silent affirmations of what you want to experience and your belief that reaching your goals is possible.

You could also create a sequence of photos and words on your phone that you can open and scroll through at any time. Even so, consider that having your vision board in one place might make you more likely to work with the board mindfully on a regular basis. In this way, you'll strengthen your motivation and optimism, which will make any problems you're facing less daunting.

RELATE TO MONEY AND TIME DIFFERENTLY

One of the most common obstacles to being creative and making big changes is the fear of running out of money and time before manifesting a vision. I have found that even people with a good amount of accumulated wealth and regular paychecks or a reliable stream of revenue can become paralyzed by the fear that they will run out of money and time.

Money is an energy that comes into your life and flows out again, ideally with more coming in than is going out! Many creative artists don't have a steady paycheck. Even after they have achieved success and built their savings, they can become very nervous about negotiations, contracts, and debt. This old pattern of worry and discomfort can be exchanged for a new habit of relating to money and time with a greater sense of creativity and open-mindedness.

Some say that time is money, and when you're anxious about missing a deadline or losing an opportunity because you took too long to act, it's important to shift your mind-set about your limitations. If you're trying to decide whether to keep going or move on, whether to abandon a project or plan, see chapter 9, "Mindful Decision Making." For now, just know that creativity can help you expand your resources—including those of money and time. You might be seeing limitations and overlooking possibilities because of your lack of experience with generating resources to support you. For example, you might not be recognizing that other people are willing to make an exchange with you, bartering something so both of you benefit. Years ago, I began jogging with my friend Carl Kugel, and it felt natural for me to answer his questions about psychology and motivation as he shared with me insights about the television and film business. We both benefited, gaining insights and knowledge that helped us in our work. As a creativity and leadership coach, I've helped artists in the fields of television and film understand how the companies they're negotiating with operate so that they can feel more confident and competent as they ask for what they want and need—and, quite often, get it.

Capital is out there, whether you generate it through taking on debt, connecting with investors, seeking funding on a site like GoFundMe, doing a fundraiser, or attaining grants and scholarships. You can also make your creative project a side gig until you build up more capital and savings. And, of course, you can turn to your Wisdom Council of Support and Creativity Support Pod to help you figure out ways to raise money.

If debt is holding you back, research into how to better manage it, whether it's taking advantage of programs to ease student loan debt or consolidating loans and finding lenders who offer lower interest rates. You can sell possessions or services that you would otherwise give away, but you have to be honest with yourself about the time involved in selling. There might be a faster and more efficient way to raise money than to sell possessions unless they're big-ticket items.

I have many people in my private practice who plan to continue to work full time as they pursue a creative project but find it difficult to carve out the time to pursue it. I try to help them see whether they're distracting themselves or procrastinating because they lack confidence and are afraid of failure. However, I also encourage them to look at how they're wasting time by binge-watching television shows or scrolling and posting on social media rather than devoting time to their more valued pursuits. I encourage them to be consistent in spending one to three hours a day working at their craft.

Personally, I find that by practicing mindfulness twice daily and doing tai chi or yoga once a day that my mind is clearer and more focused, making it easy not to lose track of time. I devote a minimum of an hour a day to my creative goals. You might record your activities for a week to discover the "distractive fat" as I call it—the blocks of time you've wasted. (iPhones have settings for generating a weekly report of how many hours you spent each day on social media, texting, messaging, email, etc.) Once you have a record of where your time is going and how much time you're wasting, you'll find yourself at a choice point where you are faced with continuing to procrastinate or reducing the fat of distraction. Then you are more likely to set up a serious schedule for cutting the fat and immersing yourself in the creative activity every day. Take mindful pauses to ask yourself, "What's most essential for me to do right now?" and "If I only had three months to live, how would I be directing my time and energy?"

Also, you'll find as you meditate and practice mindfulness more often that you develop a sense of spaciousness and a new relationship to time, experiencing it as not ticking away as quickly as it did before. You'll find it easier to see when you're frittering away time and address the underlying reasons for doing that.

IDENTIFY WINNING FORMULAS YOU CAN USE

Free from the worry of not having enough money or time, you can start to identify winning formulas you can use: blueprints for success you or someone else have benefited from. A winning formula is a structure for playing to win rather than playing to not lose, that is, playing defensively, hoping to stop the inevitable wave of change. You want to be focused on the positive—winning in a competitive situation, creating something fresh, and opening the door to new possibilities.

Are there any winning formulas from the past that you can apply to your situation today? Think back to any big changes you've made that led to good outcomes. What were the elements that added up to a successful transformation? Is there a way to approach your art, manage your resources, or find or develop creative projects that have meaning for you that worked for you in the past but that you dropped for some reason?

Back in chapter 5, "Absorbing Creative Stimulation and Getting into Open Mind Consciousness," you met James, the aspiring screenwriter who was miserable in his day job. He read some books on screenplays but also researched among his friends to find a screenwriting partner who was familiar with successful screenwriting formulas. He even started to work a few hours a week as a script reader to help judge screenplays being considered for production by a film company. James learned from the success of others—but also their failures, which helped him better understand winning screenplay formulas and their elements. My friend who was writing her second screenplay read a couple of books on screenwriting before beginning her first one so that she could begin learning her craft.

Winning formulas aren't just structures for doing the actual work you've committed to doing, however. They can also be models for getting started, moving past obstacles, and finishing up a project.

You might want to learn from role models. How did they go about doing what you want to do? Where did they start? What were their first steps? How did they approach the process of editing or refining their first draft? Where did they seek feedback? How could their winning formula work for you? Could you adapt it for yourself?

REPURPOSE A WINNING FORMULA, BREAKING THE RULES AND COMBINING IDEAS

When you're thinking of reusing a winning formula of your own or someone else's, take the time to try to identify any elements that would need to be updated or altered given any potential problems with applying the formula to what you're trying to do. Are there any rules that must change? In her book *On Becoming an Artist,* Ellen Langer suggests that when you come up against rules that seem to block your creativity, you should ask yourself this question: "Who made the rule and why?"[1] That can help you determine if the old rule applies in the current context. You might have different requirements than the inventor of the winning formula did. Also, if you were the one who came up with it, you might have changed—that formula might not be right for you anymore. You might be facing different circumstances and have a very different goal than you had previously, so the winning formula may have to be altered quite a lot. However, it might also be the case that the winning formula will work again, just as it did, but you can't see that because you're clouded by doubts.

I wrote in my book *Wise Mind, Open Mind* (2009) about a time when I was brought into a meeting of music business executives at a recording company to help them figure out what to do about a star's latest album having sluggish sales. After leading them in a meditation session, I asked them to identify winning formulas that had worked for other artists and this one in the past. They said that when the star recording artist was just beginning, she would record herself announcing who she was and stating the call letters of the radio station, which the stations would use before playing her new album. "But she wouldn't do that now," an executive said. "She's a star."

"Interesting," I thought. "Who made the rule that big stars shouldn't be approached to do radio station announcements, and why?" Aloud, I posed the question, "But why wouldn't she do that today?" It turns out that everyone assumed her ego would be bruised and that she would get angry at them for making the suggestion. "Don't you think she would be more upset by having her new album flop than she would by being asked to do marketing that in the past has been part of a winning formula?" They agreed and asked her to do the recordings. She wasn't upset in the least, and soon after the radio stations began airing the station call-outs, her album soared up the charts.

Director and screenwriter David Seltzer says, "An article that was written about me called 'The Sultan of Sob: Sob Movies, Tearjerkers and David Seltzer.' I was always interested in touching, in reaching an audience, maybe too broadly. Maybe that was a good caution the critics were giving me. But shortly after that, I wrote *The Omen*, which was also, to me, deeply about a family; to me, that was a complicated family story. It had an innocent villain, and a guilty hero: the father was a guilty hero, and the child was an innocent villain. That's a real interesting combination to work with." While some might not think to take a leap from writing dramas about families to writing a horror movie, Seltzer did.[2]

As an exercise, identify the rule in a winning formula that you think might be a problem for you. Then identify who made the rule. You might want to go back to the Return to the Scene to Change It Visualization from chapter 3 to help you identify the originator, which can make it easier to determine whether the rule must stay for the formula to work.

Also, explore the reason behind the rule. When it was created, was it based in evidence and solid reasoning or on an assumption that was never examined? Does that context for the rule still hold today or has the situation changed? Do you have a different goal or different values and priorities than the originator of the winning formula, who wrote its rules and determined what its elements are?

When a winning formula that has worked in the past no longer leads to success, it's okay to change it or even break it. A while back, entertainment attorneys in Hollywood realized that increasingly they were bringing together screenwriters and directors, packaging deals for film companies. A fee for legal services alone didn't make sense anymore given that they were doing more than they were before, so a new compensation model was in order. They began asking for 5 percent of the deal that their clients made with film production companies. Entertainment attorneys' role became more like that of agents and managers, which was much more lucrative for them.

One firm I worked with was so adept at packaging deals that I suggested they venture into brand development and assist clients with building out their brands using social media platforms. They took me up on the idea and soon had not only altered their winning formula but added onto it. When you can think along divergent lines, you are able to identify the valuable threads (what is working and what has worked in the past) and weave them together, creating a new winning formula.

Creativity allows you to combine seemingly incompatible things, and your winning formula, new or old, might be an expression of that aspect of creativity. When the Beatles recorded *Sgt. Pepper's Lonely Hearts Club Band*, a groundbreaking record that many consider to be the best rock-and-roll album of all time, they mixed songs with traditional pop structures—a winning formula for them—and songs that had unusual structures, such as "A Day in the Life." In fact, "A Day in the Life" was itself a mix of two different incomplete songs, one by John Lennon and one by Paul McCartney, connected with an instrumental section. They returned to their new winning formula, established with the *Sgt. Pepper* album, for their album *Abbey Road*, where several songs were strung together to create one piece or long song starting with "Because" and ending with "The End." You, too, might be able to combine two winning formulas—or repurpose one by adding something that on first glance doesn't seem to fit.

If you tried to create a winning formula in the past and failed, revisit what happened to see what you can learn from the experience. Maybe the timing wasn't right. Maybe you needed a collaborator. Maybe you gave up too quickly. Now might be the time to revisit something you abandoned long ago and work with it to see if you can get past whatever obstacles kept you from moving forward with it before.

You might be too attached to your winning formula as it was in the past, not recognizing that it's time to change it. In chapter 4, you met my client Kim, who didn't want to enter the digital era and strongly resisted disassembling her old, rigid formulas about how to do marketing. She needed to let go of her attachment to them as well as her attachment to seeing herself as an expert. There's an old saying: if you meet the Buddha on the road, kill him—meaning that you must be willing to kill off your attachments to your formulas and identities so you can create anew. Consider whether you have a rigid mind-set that makes you stick with the old habits that hold you back from tapping into core creativity and expressing yourself or a fluid mind-set that frees you to be spontaneous and creative.

Why do I see so many of my millennial clients remain in a job for no more than two years before they move on? The exciting and invigorating experience of getting involved in new projects and companies is a strong lure. Many freelancers say that while it can be stressful to not know when the next good opportunity will appear, they like working on projects rather than doing the same type of work in the same place, surrounded by the same people, day after day. They're always learning something, whether it's a new skill or new information, and working with new clients. Mastery can lead to boredom. Being willing to experience beginner's mind can lead to exciting discoveries about your potential, inspiring you to set new goals. Go ahead and stick with a winning formula, but be open to breaking what isn't broken to see what happens.

SEE FAILURES AND SETBACKS
AS OFFERING OPPORTUNITIES

If you're willing to detach from your winning formula and your ego's ideas about who you are and what you're not capable of, you might find that failures, setbacks, and mistakes can be viewed as "mis-takes," as Robert Resnick, an esteemed gestalt therapist, suggests: you took a particular path as a result of a choice you made, and you didn't like the outcome, but you can take a new path once you realize that you're unhappy with your results. Like a director telling an actor "Let's do another take," you can do another "take." You might not like the choices that you'll have as options, but at least you'll have options.

After singer/songwriter Joni Mitchell had a health crisis that made her unable to hold a guitar or play the piano, she took up painting. Singer and actor Julie Andrews developed nodes on her vocal cords that severely damaged her ability to sing, and surgery didn't correct the condition. Afterward, she began writing children's books to "find her voice" again, so to speak.

And you might come to discover that you feel okay with changing your original plans because you have discovered gifts that are different from the ones you aspired to discover. Music producer Val Garay, the son of a professional singer, became a guitarist and singer whose band was signed to a major label deal. "I had some success on those levels, but never major, major success," he says, "So then I went on to another area, which was engineering and producing. And everything I touched or got involved with started to happen on a major scale. So you kind of go, 'Oh, I guess, this is where I'm supposed to be.' . . . I realized I have a gift: I can hear things that most people can't. I hear a great song, I hear a great drum sound, I hear a great vocal, I just have that gifted ability. Some people do, some don't."

Garay also says, "I'm just not afraid to fuck up. And believe me, it's happened. [I went] from an album that sells in the millions, number one in over twenty countries around the world, and then the next album that I make with [the artist] sells a fraction of that. But what you have to think about is lightning strikes twice. So, if you can get to the top of the mountain once, you can get there again. People have done it."[3]

A setback may lead you in a direction you wouldn't have considered otherwise and turn out to be an opportunity for growth in a completely different area—and even great success. If you see a setback or mistake as offering possibilities, it's easier to see what those are.

Author Ellen Langer says there are four options when you make a mistake while creating a drawing (she is not only a Harvard psychologist but a painter). Your choices are as follows:

- Call it a mistake and abandon the drawing.
- Live with the mistake and keep going with the drawing.
- Try to fix the mistake by, for example, erasing it.
- Look at the mistake differently and "take advantage of it," that is, see within it the potential for a new opportunity.

She points out that most of us have been taught that the first three options are the only ones to consider.[4]

By cultivating mindfulness, you'll find it easier to let go of disappointment or harsh judgments and become curious about what the mistake offers you, which could be a doorway to a new path. Curiosity can keep you from getting stuck in the past, wishing for a different outcome than the one you experienced.

Curiosity inspires us to look at situations more holistically, seeing their complexities as well as the possibility of multiple outcomes and solutions. It also allows us to see potential in a mistake. When Eric Clapton and George Harrison were collaborating on a song, Harrison handed Clapton a handwritten piece of paper on which he'd scrawled some lyrics and the word "bridge," meaning that the next part of the song should be the bridge. Clapton misread it as "badge," the two of them laughed, and Clapton decided that should be the name of the song. Years later, he would add another element to the song "Badge": he sometimes sings a new, extra line about wondering where his badge is.[5]

TAKE A RISK RATHER THAN STAY IN YOUR LANE

Earlier, I wrote about questioning who made the rule that you feel you have to follow. Creative artists break the rules all the time. One of those rules is "stay in your lane." Great musicians often venture into film, painting, and sculpting, and even inventing devices—we wouldn't have multitrack recording or electric guitars if it weren't for guitarist Les Paul tinkering with electronics. One of the most extraordinary examples of not staying in your lane is the glamorous actor Hedy Lamarr who, during the golden age of Hollywood, was known for her beauty but overlooked for her brains and creativity. Lamarr invented a frequency-hopping communications technology for guiding torpedoes that she envisioned the Allied forces using during World War II to spot German U-boats. While sexism led the U.S. War Department to dismiss her idea and shelve it, it would turn out to serve as the foundation for technology used today for wi-fi.

Sexism, racism, ageism, ableism, and other forms of prejudice that can be huge obstacles are very real, but in creative fields, I find that many artists break unwritten rules about what someone like them "should" be doing. They find the courage to take the risk and follow their creative instincts regardless of what others might think.

And many artists continue to take creative risks and work well into their eighties and even their nineties. Often, they have made a point of taking good care of their health so they can continue to have a long health span. A colleague, mentor, and dear friend of mine, Bill O'Hanlon, who is a world-renowned Ericksonian hypnotherapist, professional speaker, and author of over fifty books, decided several years back to retire from speaking and working as a therapist. At age sixty-five, he moved into a flat in Nashville, Tennessee, and started working with songwriters and attending songwriting seminars with the goal of writing his own songs, singing, playing guitar, and performing. Thus far, he has had over twenty-five of his songs released by recording artists and several have been used in TV shows and movies. He is a great example of how it's never too late to embark on a new creative course.

Life is ever changing, and while risk-taking can lead to outcomes you don't like, you can choose to gather your resources and do your research to reduce your risk. You can also leave plenty of time to spot problems up the road and strategize about how to avoid them—and how to deal with them if you can't. Be flexible about what happens, remaining mindful, with open eyes, as you move forward with your vision. Your screenplay might become a novel. Your work as a physician or teacher might shift as you do more online or you help people heal or you educate them in a different way.

At times, your plans will be interrupted, forcing you to focus on something you didn't expect to focus on. Ronnie Landfield had to salvage his paintings and supplies from his studio after it burned, and then again years later after it flooded. "You have to just stop sometimes, he says. "I needed to shift from painting to saving and restoring my life's work," he recalls. Fortunately, with help from his sons, friends, students, and art conservators from all over the United States, he was able to save and restore just about everything.[6] Your interruption might be financial problems, health issues, or something else, but however big the setback is, remember that the unexpected will happen. The wheel of life will turn and better luck will come around, but you might have to set aside your plans to a large degree until you deal with your challenges in the present. Keep in touch with your creativity, though, even if it's only for a short amount of time each day. What you might find is that the detour takes you on a completely new path. As I said earlier, a setback can offer an opportunity. If you take it, you might find that your new lane is even better than the old one.

And keep in mind that it's easier to accept risk when you're focused on what you might discover and create rather than what you have lost and what you might lose in the future. Maintain a forward focus. Practice adventurous risk taking so you can tame any lingering fears that keep you stuck in worries about the potential problems you might face. Think about some activities that can take you out of your comfort zone and start to do them. Remember the woman who invested a little in the stock market to help her feel more comfortable being an "investor" and someone who had money to invest? Take some small chances and soon you'll find the confidence to take some larger ones.

PERSEVERE AND BE PATIENT

Often, ideas come as mere snippets. Academy Award–winning director Steven Soderbergh's career-establishing, Palm D'Or–winning film *Sex, Lies, and Videotape* began with these brief notes for a potential screenplay that he wrote in a notebook: "A film about deception and lost earrings . . . Everybody has a past . . . Friend on the couch. Affair with the wife."[7] His story is a good reminder of the value of a notebook, but of course, keeping a notebook and pen or your cell phone near you at all times so you can capture ideas is a good habit to get into. When I swim in the ocean, I often get downloads of ideas. As soon as I get out of the water, even before I towel off, I record them. An idea that seems too brief and lacking detail can be built upon and might become a full-fledged creative work if you don't give up on it too early.

The Jackie DeShannon version of the song "Bette Davis Eyes" that producer Val Garay was inspired by is quite different from the one he produced for Kim Carnes that won a Grammy Award because he zeroed in on what he loved about the song rather than what he disliked about the recording. He explains, "I sat down with an acoustic guitar, because I loved the lyrics of the song, but I hated the way it was done. . . . I sat down with an acoustic guitar and started playing 'Bette Davis Eyes' kind of like a three-chord folk song, slowed down from that demo. And then I went to [keyboard player] Bill Cuomo and said, listen, create me a lick."[8] From there, the hit version of the song took form. But it never would have happened if Val Garay had let himself become distracted by all the aspects of the original version that didn't appeal to him. He built on what he felt worked.

Another reason to be patient and persevere is because it can be tempting to abandon a goal if you're convinced your idea is too crazy and "out there." The hit television show *Seinfeld* could be described as a show about nothing, which sounds ridiculous—but it's a crazy idea that turned out to be brilliant. George Martin and Paul McCartney assembled strips made up of random snippets of recording tape with various sounds on them, and the result ended up on the Beatles' song "Tomorrow Never Knows." Singer/songwriter Freddie Mercury began to write a rock ballad only to add on an operatic section that turned out to be an element in the Queen song "Bohemian Rhapsody" that helped make it a massive hit.

If you're unsure about the feasibility of your idea, don't give up before getting some feedback both from within—from your intuition—and from people who encourage you in your creative projects and transformations. Creative artists know that the crazy idea is often the brilliant one—or leads to the brilliant one.

As you learn to trust the core creativity process, using doorways into open mind and adopting habits and mind-sets of highly creative people, you'll be less quick to talk yourself out of pursing a crazy idea that might be the foundation of something great. Biases and preconceived notions will have less of a hold on you. You'll start entertaining new ideas that arise in your awareness, even if they do not seem viable at first—even if they seem to be just snippets of ideas or ideas far too "out there" to be worth pursuing.

If you look at your idea and think, "I don't know if this will work because no one's ever done this before," it might be that no one has tried it because it's a terrible idea—but it might be that yours is a fresh, terrific idea. You don't have to reinvent the wheel, but you might do something much more innovative than you think you're capable of doing. "Crazy" can start to look very different as you sit, mindfully present, and connect with your intuition core creativity in open mind to gain more insights into where you might go with your idea, building on it.

I led an Art of Leadership retreat that several Apple employees and executives attended. Morale at the company was very low under the leadership of John Scully. There were rumors that the company's iconic and visionary leader, Steve Jobs, might return, but many dismissed them as unrealistic. During the retreat, I instructed the Apple staffers to visualize what would happen if Jobs were to return, simply as a way of breaking down a firewall to their core creativity. At first, they resisted this "crazy" idea, saying, "What's the point? It'll never happen." Over the next hour or so, enthusiasm and hope swelled as the visualization that put them in open mind planted a seed of possibility that rooted, sprouted, and grew. They reported they experienced the level of enthusiasm they had experienced back in the days when Jobs was the visionary leader at the helm of Apple. I explained that whether or not Jobs did come back, what they had learned was that they could shift their mindset without changing their external circumstances and that open mind could lead to core creativity and innovation. Low morale dampens creativity, and I knew they needed to recognize their own power to become innovative again. They had to experience the portal of open mind, and the sense of expansiveness, vitality, and possibility that would restore their faith that they could come up with specific, actionable ideas. As it turns out, the "crazy" idea I led the team to consider turned out not to be so crazy after all: Jobs returned to run Apple.

Necessity is the mother of invention, as the saying goes, but you don't have to wait until a crisis to be creative and look to other models of success and even to "crazy" ideas to improve your situation and your chances of reaching your goals. In Tibetan Buddhism, there is a way of teaching, introduced by the author and teacher Trungpa Rinpoche, called "crazy wisdom." When one is practicing crazy wisdom, one is encouraged to expand limited and fixed beliefs about what is and what is not.

Be patient as you go through a process of saying good-bye to the old and hello to the new. The COVID pandemic upended long-standing work formulas for many people. They were no longer traveling to the office, meeting and working in person with other people, buying lunch and eating out, making arrangements for kids to be supervised after they got out of school and before their parents got home from their workplace, and so on. It's understandable that many employers and employees—and students and teachers—yearned for a return to the comfort of the familiar, old ways. However, many thrived in the "new normal," forcing others to consider taking the best of the old and the new and going forward with a hybrid way of doing work or school.

Patience is also required in building skills to achieve your vision. Many years ago, I saw Robin Williams perform at a club in Los Angeles, long before he became a famous comic. He was doing improv with a partner from the comedy group Off the Wall and completely bombing. No one was cracking a smile, and it was uncomfortable sitting there waiting for the team to finally make a joke land or save us all a lot of agony by leaving the stage. I could see from the program that

Williams was scheduled to come on stage again later in the evening as a solo comic and thought, "How is this guy going to come back from that awful performance?" I almost left the theater early, but, for some reason, decided to see if the rest of the show was any better. When Robin Williams performed again, he was so hilarious my face hurt from laughing. I walked out of there thinking how glad I was that he hadn't let his failure stop him from performing a second time that night—and that I'd given him a second chance. Later, he would do some marvelously comic performances improvising with partners, and seemed to have learned something from his past failures rather than giving up and vowing to only work solo from then on. Comics need to work out their timing in front of audiences, and I'm guessing Robin Williams didn't find it easy to persevere at his craft given that when he failed, he did so in a very public way. Still, he had to be bad before he could get good. He had to be patient and persevere.

Dennis Quaid said, "I've always had to really work at everything. . . . I know many, many talented people who gave up or lost interest or whatever it was, or believed what people were saying about them. And I just felt like I would always have to work harder than anybody else. I didn't feel like I really had any kind of like, amazing gifts. . . . I just thought I really had to work harder." His hard work paid off in the movie *Great Balls of Fire*, in which he played rock-and-roll icon Jerry Lee Lewis: "I got Jerry Lee Lewis mentoring me," Quaid said, "and I had a year to prepare for it. At that time, I didn't play piano. I was like thirty-three years old, and I practiced the piano twelve hours a day."

The perseverance you draw on can come from another area of life, such as work. Quaid says that for him, "I guess it comes from when I was like a door-to-door salesman, selling newspaper subscriptions or Amway or Fuller brushes. It takes guts, knock on somebody's door cold and try to sell them something. And from that, I think I kind of got used to that fear just getting out of the way. . . . And being an actor, and being in the arts, you get so many nos. You develop a thick skin towards it. If you don't have confidence, get some anyway! Confidence just generates more confidence. It brings success, which brings more confidence."[9]

Perseverance means not giving up if one idea after another doesn't pan out. It means you continue with your creative process. When it comes to writing songs, Dennis Quaid says he finds it can take "nine ideas to get one good idea. . . . You're like throwing the spaghetti up there on the wall, seeing what sticks and what attracts your eye."[10] If you record the ideas that come to you—for example, writing about them or drawing them in a journal—you can revisit them later to see if they speak to you. You might be surprised by what a fresh perspective can reveal.

Director Amy Ziering says of the filmmaking process, "Sometimes we literally call a brainstorming meeting with staff, describe what we are struggling with, and have people toss out whatever ideas they might have. Even if we don't run with anything broached, sometimes those ideas open up new venues of thinking that hadn't occurred to us on our own. . . . Often, my best ideas come when I'm not actively thinking about work at all."[11]

It's said that it takes ten thousand hours to achieve mastery, which means you'll have to develop a lot of patience, because even if you were to work at something eight hours a day, it would take three and a half years to become a master. Fortunately, mindfulness practice will help you relate to time differently, as I said, which will grow your patience. And you can also try the following Mindful Patience Meditation.

MINDFUL PATIENCE MEDITATION

Sit in a relaxed and comfortable position and rest your gaze at the tip of your nose (keeping your eyes open or closed, whichever is most comfortable) as you focus on your breath. Now bring to the foreground of your mind's awareness a project that you worked on where you became frustrated and impatient, causing you to complete the project with regret and discomfort with the process or to drop the project altogether. Maybe you were too impulsive or wound it up too quickly, not giving the project the time it needed. Now go back, and this time see yourself mentally repeating, "There's plenty of time." Take long, slow breaths and exhale slowly to entrain your brain and nervous system to slow down. This will quiet your impulsivity and sense of urgency.

As you feel yourself slowing down and resting, notice how you feel in your body. Connect to that energy, bringing your awareness to it. Observe just how easy it is for you to move from impatience into patience. Pay attention to how your nervous system is comfortably settling down to a slower pace of operation.

Now, remaining connected to the new energy of patience, continue to inhale and exhale in long, slow breaths, and as you exhale, think to yourself, "Patience pays off. My rhythm. My timing." Continue to repeat these statements to yourself as you experience the calming rhythm of your breathing. Notice that as you draw in breath, exhale, and rest, you are experiencing a perfect circle of breathing.

Continue with the meditation until you feel you're ready to end it.

REMAIN TRUE TO YOUR VALUES AND PRIORITIES

As I mentioned, many millennials are negotiating with employers for a shorter work week so they can have a higher quality of life. They are rejecting the old "work around the clock to prove your dedication" formula. Baby boomers facing retirement are asking themselves whether they want to continue working full time, retire from paid work, or work fewer hours at a career they love. Without a plan to grind to a halt, they're considering what they want to do at sixty-five or seventy-five, and whether they need to get paid for it and, if so, how much.

What are your values and priorities? If you're plugging away at your day job and spending very little time in activities you say you value, mindfulness practice will make it easier to catch yourself enmeshed in the fat of distraction or in a violation of your values.

My health is very important to me, in no small part because my family tree has branch after branch populated by people who developed cardiovascular disease and diabetes at a young age and suffered a reduced quality of life and a premature death as a result. Over the years, I've changed my diet to be more plant-based; I've meditated, practiced yoga and tai chi. And I've had a very active exercise routine of hiking, swimming, bike riding, rollerblading, skiing, and running my entire adult life. At seventy, I have no major health issues, but that's because mindfulness practice has helped me recognize when I'm not being true to what I value. And mindfulness has helped me be compassionate toward myself and get back on a healthy path very quickly rather than retreat into denial to avoid feelings of shame and disappointment.

You might be much younger than I am yet already experiencing the effects of too many late nights, poor eating habits, excessive drinking, too little high-quality sleep, and so on. If that's the case, how long do you plan to continue keeping your health low on your list of priorities? Think about changes you could start making today to give yourself more stamina and lower your risk of developing a health problem because you pushed yourself too hard. Stress makes it even harder for your body to stay healthy. Are you managing stress well? If you were to put off for twenty-five years any changes that would improve your health, where do you think you would be? If you don't like to contemplate the outcome of continuing as you have been, at what point are you going to make changes?

As an exercise, imagine that instead of putting off your health until some undefined point in the future, you have set a clear intention to exercise and eat and sleep well now. Project how you will feel in the future having taken a more healthy and balanced approach to your health. I was newly licensed as a psychotherapist at twenty-six years old and made a conscious decision to map out a pathway toward health and well-being rather than to succumb to the intergenerational disease that my father and family relatives all were suffering with. You don't have to wait until you develop a health problem. You can decide to prioritize your health now.

In addition to valuing your health, you might value creative time, spiritual practice time, time with family and friends, and time to think, dream, and envision what you'd like to experience and accomplish. What will it feel like in the future if you don't live according to your priorities and values and create the life you want for yourself?

Asked about playing with his band, the Sharks, actor Dennis Quaid said,

> What really matters is whether I think it's good or not, and most of what really matters is the experience of creating it. And that's why we were originally doing it. Because we find joy in that. Way before I was getting paid, I was finding joy in writing songs or joy in doing acting. . . . You just let your mind open, and something comes through. And that's where the true enjoyment or that joy comes from, or that satisfaction. Not from any kind of awards or anything afterwards, or trophies—you know, alright, nice, whatever. . . . It's all in the doing of it in the moment. It always comes back to being in the moment.[12]

In the moment, pay attention to how you feel. Are you happy? Fulfilled? Enthusiastic? You might discover that activities you felt would be rewarding aren't anymore—or never really were! Ask yourself, "Is this activity or type of work nourishing to my soul?" If not, stop doing what is no longer nourishing and search for what is or could be more fulfilling. Now is the time to rework your schedule to reflect your true priorities.

ACKNOWLEDGE YOUR SUCCESSES TO MAINTAIN YOUR MOTIVATION

When you've completed a project or even just a challenging part of it, be present with the feeling of satisfaction and pride. Take a moment to look at your completed paper printed out, the food you've cooked, or whatever it is that's tangible evidence that you persevered and met your goals. I've worked with a lot of people who wanted to pursue a dream but felt they couldn't quit their day jobs, and I tell them they don't have to—at least, not initially.

Mindfulness practice helps you remain fully present as you experience the moment instead of distracting yourself with thoughts. Journal about your creative successes, analyzing all that you did right. And talk with supportive creative people who will acknowledge your creativity and take it seriously. They can remind you of your strengths, which can be helpful for building your confidence and pulling yourself out of a spell of insecurity. You might even recall some of the compliments you have received over the years and write them on a vision board or in a journal to review them from time to time, especially when you're feeling stuck or you're doubting yourself.

A colleague of mine who had worked in the field of psychoanalysis far longer than I, and who had written several books, developed severe depression. She called me from her office one afternoon and told me she didn't see any purpose in living any longer as she could not get herself focused to see patients or to write something. I closed my eyes, tuned in to my intuition and core creativity, and in my mind, I saw her listening to her patients as they smiled at her and she nodded. I opened my eyes and suggested that she make ten phone calls to patients she saw long ago and ask them if they would share with her stories of how her analysis with them had positively affected their lives. She followed through with my idea and was utterly astonished by the glowing details of enormous life changes and shifts they reported experiencing as a result of psychoanalysis with her. As she was gathering these stories, I instructed her to call me daily and to share them with me over the phone. After several such calls, I could hear in her voice a newfound energy. In fact, her spirit became so uplifted that she applied for—and received—a grant that would allow her to write a book.

CHANGE THE SPACE YOU'RE IN

You might have a favored place for meditating, creating, or both, but the more you build your mindstrength to shift into open mind, the more easily you'll be able to tap into your creativity and intuition and download ideas and insights wherever you are. I have met many musicians and songwriters who have become very adept at writing and playing new songs and music in different spaces: in planes, tour buses, taxis, hotel rooms, and so on. Always have with you tools for recording your ideas, whether it's a journal and pen or an app on your phone. I've known people to dictate emails to themselves on a cell phone to record ideas when their pen ran out of ink. Others have sung melodies and words into a recording app. When the muse appears, be ready to meet it.

Also, travel exposes you to new stimulation you can absorb, whether it's the culture, sights, and sounds of a small town or a big city within a couple hours from you. Think about booking a retreat for doing creative work, even if it's simply housesitting for someone who is going on vacation. There's something about changing your physical space and locale that can shift your mind-set. For one thing, it can free you of distractions, whether it's the people and animals you live with, projects around your home, or the refrigerator! Many writers have checked into a hotel to write, completely uninterrupted.

One of my coaching clients, a visual artist, was feeling very burned out and decided to take a trip to visit some Tibetan and Indian monasteries to experience the richness of the spiritual traditions, art, and colors while also spending time in meditation. At a monastery, he went into open mind and found his imagination flooded with new ideas. You can try working on creative projects far away from home or nearby—in cafes, parks, museums, and your yard or garden, or by a lake, river, or ocean.

Alter your surroundings at home if you're unable to travel. Move furniture around, switch out the lighting, bring in nature with houseplants or photographs of mountains and beaches, and use music and essential oils or fresh flowers that provide an olfactory experience. Anything that awakens the senses can help you be less constricted by your analytical, rational mind so that it serves you rather than dictates your thought processes.

At home, if the energy for creative output is not flowing at your usual battle station, move to another spot. Often, when I am stuck or blocked, I will move my workstation from inside my home office to the back Zen garden. Throughout the day, I may move from the home office to the Zen garden to my living room, where there are large windows and plenty of natural light. Sometimes, I'll even work sitting on top of my bed, which reminds me of back when I was a kid and would be sick at home and dutifully doing my homework in bed, as I'd promised my mother.

GET ORGANIZED IN A WAY THAT WORKS FOR YOU

Respect your habits and rhythms as you organize your time and possessions. You might have to do some research to figure out what organizing systems will stick for you and help you find what you need and get to work promptly rather than chasing down tools you need that you left who knows where. Simple systems that don't require a lot of brain power to use, along with the habit of checking your calendar first thing every morning and straightening up your workspace as an end-of-the-day ritual, can help you avoid feeling scattered and being less productive than you could be.

Musical composer and steel drummer Jonathan Scales says,

> In my early years, before I became a full-time musician, I worked at a factory that manufactured CDs and DVDs, and I noticed the way that the production ran . . . and the way they organized everything. They organized by which orders were hotter than others and needed to be out the door faster. . . . My organization, my schedule, is different than a lot of musicians'. It's more like a business. . . . It's really easy to become overwhelmed because, especially as an artist, there's no end to it. . . . There's always something you can do. . . . You could be practicing. You could be writing. . . . That business structure helps me to compartmentalize my day.[13]

ESTABLISH ROUTINES AND RITUALS, RESPECTING YOUR NATURAL RHYTHMS

In the 2013 documentary *History of the Eagles*, Glenn Frey talked about when he lived upstairs from Jackson Browne in the Echo Park neighborhood of Los Angeles back in the 1970s. Frey would hear the whistle of Jackson Browne's teakettle downstairs and, soon, the sound of Browne on the piano, playing the first verse and chorus of a song twenty times, then the second verse twenty times, then going back to the beginning and playing from the top, over and over. Frey says this experience taught him that waiting around for inspiration to hit was not the only way to write songs. Instead, it could involve "elbow grease, time, thought, persistence." His neighbor's discipline inspired him, and from playing small gigs, Frey ended up playing arenas and having hit records with the Eagles as a guitarist and songwriter.[14]

When we perform rituals, we move from simple, predictable, mundane actions to more seriously focused, disciplined ones. Daily rituals can reduce anxiety.[15] The Academy Award–winning documentary film director Amy Ziering goes to bed each evening between 9 and 10 p.m., rises at 5 a.m. or earlier to have time to eat breakfast, meditate, and work out, and is at her desk by 8 a.m. She remembers what she learned from her father: hard work and daily discipline go a long way toward success.[16] Repeating a daily sequence of activities becomes a container for the sprouting of new ideas.

It's common for creative artists to listen to music as they paint, sculpt, draw, write, and so on. Music often shifts us from being analytical and logical to being more intuitive, open, and imaginative, so artists and people in creative fields will often play music while working or before starting work. Listening to music that quiets the analytical mind can set the stage for experiencing open mind and creativity. The sixties activist, prolific author, and California politician Tom Hayden once told me that when he was writing his book *Reunion: A Memoir* (1989) that he played U2's *Joshua Tree* album nonstop as a background support for his writing. Music can be a powerful aid for staying focused and alert and in the creative zone.[17]

A successful and highly respected clothing designer I was coaching shared with me that when she feels pressured to deliver new clothing concepts to her team of designers, she will perform the following ritual:

She'll tell her assistant to hold all calls, put her cell phone on silent, close her office door, and make herself a cup of mint tea. She'll take the tea with her as she sits down on a small meditation rug that lies in the corner of her office next to a small sacred *puja*—a Sanskrit word for holy or sacred table. Her puja has incense, beautifully scented candles, some bowls filled with water, and beautiful framed pictures of nature, loved ones, and herself at one of many red-carpet design openings. The latter recaptures the energy and emotions of experiencing that moment in time when she felt and experienced herself to be totally alive and in the flow or zone of creativity. After meditating for 15 to 30 minutes, she goes into a state of open mind. The ritual is what she calls a road map or path to her inner creative well of being. She knows and trusts it, saying it has never failed her.

Waking up early turns out to be very common among highly creative people—at least according to my experience and a book called *Daily Rituals: How Artists Work* (2013), which author Mason Currey says was inspired by his curiosity about whether other creatives woke up early and were at their most productive in the morning. He learned that Ernest Hemingway was among those who rose at 5:30 a.m., which we might not expect considering his reputation for enjoying nightlife! In fact, most of the creative luminaries featured in the book reported that their routine was to get up early to work, and at some point after lunch, take a walk, work again, have dinner, and retire early. And author Henry Miller would work in the morning, nap, then continue his writing, often through the evening. Later in his career, he felt that working after lunch was "unnecessary and even counterproductive."[18] It's important to work with your natural rhythms. If you can do the most difficult tasks that require the most creativity and concentration first, you can do less challenging tasks later in the day.

And, of course, some highly creative people are night owls. Musicians, who perform at night, may not get up until much later in the day. However, the professionals get down to business right away, even if the day starts late in the evening.

Your morning ritual might start like painter Ronnie Landfield's: coffee on the porch before heading into his workspace to get down to business.[19] Director and screenwriter David Seltzer says,

> Starbucks used to be a big part of [my morning routine]. . . . I was always the first person there. It used to be 4:30 in the morning. I helped [the

workers] put the chairs out and they thought I must be somebody who sleeps in his car until ultimately we got to know each other. That was a real social part of my day, particularly, when I was living with my kids, because I could get out while they were still asleep, get my coffee, and get myself settled in, do some work. And that's changed now. I don't have any rituals for working. I do always have to have a cup of coffee to kick-start myself. Beyond that, it's put your ass in the chair and make something happen.[20]

He also says, "Sometimes I need something to prime myself. I call it reentry—I think you're calling it entering the creative zone." Seltzer will write a letter to himself about his work from the day before and will remind himself of why he's writing. "Rather than sitting here and starting with the end of yesterday's work, I'll give myself a review, and in it, there will always be a new thought and new idea, and that's enough to kick-start the writing." If you do this, he says, "you can generate some heat before you strike."[21]

Another writer I know reads what she wrote in her last writing session so that she can immerse herself in the flow again. These two writers are examples of what works for one person might not work for another. If your ritual is effective for you, it doesn't matter if it fits someone else's idea of how you're supposed to turn on the tap to creative flow. Chris Choy, an Academy Award–nominated documentary filmmaker and professor at NYU and other universities, told me she sometimes stays in the shower for close to an hour when awaiting new ideas or she feels blocked on a film project. If you can pay the water bill, why not?[22]

SETTING GOALS AND STAYING ON TRACK

If you don't have a ritual for beginning your day, you might start it by visualizing yourself accomplishing what you are planning to do and then visualize yourself arriving at the completion, maybe imagining yourself focusing on your three or four most difficult and important tasks. Do you know what they are each day? Identifying them might help you stay on course. You might also commit to a minimum output for the day. For example, if you're a writer, commit to writing a certain number of words. Ernest Hemingway kept a chart on which he recorded whether he was keeping up with his daily word count goal.[23]

Goals that are measurable and concrete can help you stay focused even when distractions surround you. In the book *The Success Principles* (2005, with Janet Switzer), author Jack Canfield suggested setting minimum, target, and outrageous goals.[24] Your outrageous goal might be to begin doing speaking engagements. A minimum goal might be to write out three potential titles of speeches you could give and list the major points you would want to make. A target goal might be to actually write the speeches, refine the titles, and draft descriptions that you could work into a marketing strategy to get booked to speak.

Whatever your big goal is, you have to break it down into smaller goals, and you will also want to become clear on what the real goal is. I get coaching clients who tell me their goal is to become a billionaire (years ago, clients would aspire to be a millionaire, but inflation has had its effect!). I ask them to identify what are the first three steps they need to take today, this week, or this month to set in motion the big action plan to accomplish that goal. First, I suggest, declaring what the goal is has a powerful effect on commitment to it. If you continue to affirm your goal, it's easier to avoid distractions and to feel your dedication. Also, in declaring your goal, you might want to explore what the true goal is. Is it really to acquire a certain amount of money, or is it to enjoy the life that having that amount of money would afford you? Some of my clients want to experience financial success and then shift into philanthropy. Others (not necessarily the aspiring billionaires) want to make their mark on the world or to untether themselves from a job so they can spend their time doing what has meaning for them. Some people love their jobs so much that they would like to alleviate some of the stressors related to working but continue the work for as long as possible.

I've known many wealthy people who spent a year or two traveling or enjoying their favorite everyday activities but then started to devote their time to something that gave them purpose, meaning, and a sense of connection to other people and to something larger than themselves. Ken Dychtwald, my old friend and colleague from the Esalen Institute who recently was the subject of both a wonderful PBS television series and a book, calls this focus "Life's Third Age." It's a time to reorganize and to prioritize one's values, meaning, and purpose as we go forth playing to win in the third act of our lives. I once asked a much-celebrated actor I met at a party what she was doing. She said she had fired her business manager of thirty years and was doing her own investing and loving it. She didn't need to make more money, but she enjoyed doing it. She was also enthusiastic about renovating a room in her house where she wanted to spend time in creative pursuits outside of acting. These goals clearly excited her.

Over my years of working with highly creative people in a variety of fields, I have found that one of the biggest challenges to retaining a focus on goals is mental illness and brain differences such as ADHD. Next, you'll learn about how meditation and medication can play important roles in helping you access your core creativity and use it effectively, no matter what your aspirations are.

Chapter Eight

Meditation, Medication, and Psychedelics

It was the late 1960s, and I was a student at the University of Massachusetts, Amherst, taking classes at Smith, Hampshire, and Amherst Colleges in Buddhist and consciousness studies. My anxiety about doing well in school was keeping me from sleeping well, so I went to my school's mental health center for help. There, a social worker told me she could refer me to a psychiatrist who would give me medication, or to a clinical psychologist who had recently returned from a trip to India and could teach me meditation. The Beatles had recently returned from a retreat in Rishikesh, where they had studied Transcendental™ Meditation with the Maharishi Mahesh Yogi, and I immediately knew what my answer was: I wanted to try meditation.

I told the social worker, "I must be one of the only students you've seen who asked for meditation rather than medication," and she laughed and said that was true. She also mentioned that for anxiety, both paths seemed to be effective. I knew I wanted meditation, not because I had any concerns about the drugs a psychiatrist would prescribe but because I wanted a lasting solution and hoped meditation would be it.

Flash forward to today: I continue to use meditation to control my anxiety, but I also recommend to my patients that they consider medication if I think they might benefit from it. And I refer them to a psychiatrist, a medical doctor with expertise in this area.

MENTAL HEALTH AND YOUR CREATIVITY

A wide range of diagnoses fall under the umbrella of mental health conditions, including ADHD, generalized anxiety disorder, clinical depression, schizophrenia, bipolar disorder, and more. With all of these, there is, too often, stigma because of misunderstandings about the nature of these brain differences and the people who have them. For example, people with ADHD aren't necessarily hyperactive, and there are many types of depression with different causes. Many people with mental health conditions can lead very productive lives if they can reliably and consistently access the help they need.

As I said earlier, while there is evidence of a connection between some mental health conditions and creativity, it's very weak. There's no evidence to support the idea that becoming more creative can cause mental illness, and if you have a mental health condition, it's highly unlikely that your creativity is a result of it. Treatment might make you more creative and productive.

Kay Jamison Redfield, a clinical psychologist on the faculty at Johns Hopkins University School of Medicine, is an expert on bipolar disorder (and she has this condition). In her book *Touched with Fire: Manic Depressive Illness and the Artistic Temperament* (1993), she writes about renowned artists and creative people who had mood disorders. Jamison Redfield believes that a change of mood state may be the key to triggering a creative state rather than the negative mood itself.[1] That might explain any connection between mood disorders and creativity. For many, creativity has transformative powers—which is important to remember if you are prone to dark moods.

Singer/songwriter Leonard Cohen was quoted in *Rolling Stone* magazine in 2016 as saying, "Depression has often been the general background of my daily life. . . . My feeling is that whatever I did was in spite of that, not because of it. It wasn't the depression that was the engine of my work. That was just the sea I swam in."[2] Bruce Springsteen has said that depression or sadness has helped him in his songwriting to some degree: "You got to have friction and tension, something to push up against. Every writer needs that. . . . So if the triumphant part of the song was going to feel real and not just hacked out, I had to have something I was pushing up against. I just understood that balance.[3] He has also spoken candidly about undergoing therapy. He told interviewer

Bob Love, "The talking cure—it works. But you've got to commit yourself to a process. And I was pretty good at doing that. I enjoyed the investigative examination of issues in my life that I didn't understand. I learned a lot and therefore was able to exploit what I had learned and turn it into a real life."[4] And Springsteen has been candid about using antidepressants.

In fact, many creative artists throughout history have suffered from depression, including Jimi Hendrix, Ernest Hemingway, Joni Mitchell—and more recently, artists such as Ariana Grande and Lady Gaga have spoken out about their battles with this difficult condition. Even creative leaders like Winston Churchill and Abraham Lincoln had depression, yet they were able to pen speeches that powerfully inspired people at times of great fear and dread.

If you don't feel creative or inclined to work because of depression, it might be better to address your mood first. Screenwriter and director David Seltzer says, "I have to put myself in a positive frame of mind if I'm wounded. I'm not going to write from that place [of sadness] because that's a broad brush, and I need to be much more fine-tuned. Writing is my way of breaking the grip of sadness." He acknowledges that what works for him might not work for others, saying, "I think a lot of artists maybe do some great work when they're feeling their pain. I feel my pain enough so that I can say, 'Okay, you go over there. You'll be there when I'm done. I need to lift myself out by doing this [writing].'"[5] If you feel depressed, you may be less inclined to engage in creative activities. In that case, do something that will make you feel better—for example, you could reach out and make contact with friends, collaborators, your Wisdom Council of Support, Creativity Support Pod, or therapist. They can encourage you to do what's needed to shift your mood and reconnect with your creativity. Doing a meditation like the ones in this book can help, too.

Also, recognize that meditation or medication isn't an either/or choice. Ideally, regardless of whether you use medications, you will make some lifestyle changes to better manage your moods and mental processes. During the seventies and eighties as a young psychotherapist, I was plagued with severe bouts of anxiety and depression, so I studied mindfulness meditation with Jack Kornfield and Joseph Goldstein from the Insight Meditation Society in Barre, Massachusetts, and undertook many of their ten-day Vipassana retreats. Jack founded the

Spirit Rock Meditation Center in Woodacre, California, taught there, and would frequently refer to me some of his meditation students in Southern California who, after undergoing an intensive retreat, came out feeling worse rather than feeling better. At the Zen Center Los Angeles, some students who had completed ten-day Zen "sesshins" (retreats) would feel deeply depressed, discouraged, and highly anxious instead of uplifted and blissful like their peers at the retreats—which I learned when the students came to me for help. I struggled with offering the best forms of psychotherapies of the day but often came up short at being able to shift these patients from severe depression and anxiety toward a better state of being.

Then, in 1988, the Eli Lilly company began marketing a new medication called Prozac. When I began to introduce this SSRI, referring patients to psychiatrists to consult with them about these medications, I found my meditation patients returning from meditation retreats reporting new feelings of peacefulness, calm, and clarity of mind, not just upon coming home but as a result of carrying over the meditation into daily practice. Very soon after that, one of my psychiatrist colleagues, Dr. Mark Epstein from New York City, who was also a mindfulness meditator, wrote an article called "Awakening through Prozac" (1993) in *Tricycle* magazine, reporting similar findings to what I had observed in my practice: some meditators who had a strong history of severe anxiety and depressive disorders found that using an SSRI, they experienced dramatic improvements in their meditation practice. He also found that the meditative experience significantly improves for meditators with a high amount of anxiety and a greater than average propensity for depression when they use antidepressant medication.

Whether or not you use medication for improving your mental wellness, I recommend establishing a mindfulness meditation practice. It's very hard to make changes when you're not aware of your habits. Mindfulness practice is highly effective for developing greater self-awareness and can be like rocket fuel for positive transformation. Then, too, you'll want other lifestyle interventions such as exercise, using a therapeutic 10,000-lux light box for seasonal affective disorder (if you have that issue), spiritual practice, and spending time in nature in your wellness toolbox. Also, nature time might jump-start your creativity. A study in 2012 showed that after four days of hiking in nature, the fifty-six test subjects performed 50 percent better on a test of creative problem solving.[6]

You can also talk with a functional medicine doctor (also known as an integrative medicine doctor), a therapist, or a psychologist, as well as a nutritionist, about whether you would benefit from an altered diet and nutritional supplements. I know from working with people who have depression that 5-HTP sometimes works as an antidepressant that's as effective as an SSRI (like Zoloft and Prozac), and SAM-e sometimes can be a substitute for a dopamine-reuptake antidepressant (Wellbutrin is an example). Many of my colleagues in London and Germany who do music rehabilitation therapy use it as an antidepressant and see terrific results. I've also had patients successfully use the following to treat anxiety or mild depression:

- GABA
- St. John's Wort
- 5-HTP
- L-tryptophan
- L-theanine
- kava kava
- chamomile
- magnesium
- melatonin
- CBD (CBD oil and tinctures with or without low doses of THC can be very effective for treating anxiety, and also sleep disturbances and bodily pain, from what I've seen.)

There may be other nutritional supplements that will help you develop and maintain positive mood states (such as vitamin D). Nutritional testing might prove helpful in identifying deficits that you can address through food and supplements, especially if you've been eating poorly or drinking a lot, which can strip you of some nutrients that could affect your mood. Be frank with your team of health and wellness professionals about what medications and supplements you are taking in case they interfere with each other—for example, a medication might make it harder to absorb certain nutrients.

Many of my patients are resistant to medication because they believe that medications are bad while natural interventions are good. I tell them that the same universe that gave us chamomile tea gave us the salts used to make lithium (a medication used to prevent mania and stabilize moods in people with bipolar disorder). Yes, lithium was manufactured in a laboratory, but that doesn't mean your body will be harmed by it. However, your body may be harmed by what you do and what happens to you with uncontrolled bipolar disorder. Believe me, a lot of the people I work with have strong feelings about beginning to use pharmaceutical medications—even those who use street drugs that have dubious origins! If I feel it's safe for them, I will give them two choices: the first is that they can devote sixty to ninety days to using nutritional and lifestyle interventions to see how that goes, working with a functional medicine doctor (also known as an integrative medicine doctor) and a nutritionist and doing mindfulness meditation practice. The second is that I can refer them to a psychiatrist who can determine whether they need medication, and, if so, what type.

Some people who have anxiety or mild depression do well with lifestyle changes alone, but many call me before that sixty or ninety days is up to ask for a referral to a psychiatrist. Many of my patients have found that medication jump-starts their ability to establish new lifestyle habits, helps them sleep better, gives them more energy and focus, and contributes to greater creative output.

Finally, consider that you might be one of those people who need medication because of your genetic inheritance. Some people's bodies naturally create the proper chemistry to regulate their bodies and moods, but some people's bodies can't. If you have type-2 diabetes, you might be able to reverse it with diet and lifestyle changes, but maybe not. If your pancreas couldn't be prodded into functioning properly again, you wouldn't hesitate to use medications to keep yourself alive and functioning, so don't automatically dismiss medication as a potential treatment for your mental health condition.

Also, your psychological condition might be rooted in underlying, unresolved trauma, including intergenerational trauma passed down from parent to child generation after generation.[7] As you begin to heal from that trauma, you might discover you don't need medications, might be able to reduce your dosages, or might have to take your medications indefinitely. Whatever the case, you aren't responsible for your genes or the trauma you experienced or inherited. Why should you suffer needlessly when there may be medications that would make a huge difference in your quality of life?

That said, medications, even if paired with lifestyle changes and a new diet, won't rewire your brain, even though they will affect your brain chemistry. Ideally, you will also develop new mind-sets and habits that support creativity and well-being, taking a multipronged approach to mental wellness.

WHAT'S RIGHT FOR YOU

People's bodies are unique. Just because it's natural doesn't mean it will work well for you with no side effects, and the medication that works for one person might not work well for another. While psychiatrists would love to be able to do testing to find the right medication for you before prescribing, Western medicine isn't always there yet. That said, if you have ADHD, you can do pharmacogenetic testing to discover which ADHD medication is likely to be best for you based on your genetics. You can also get tested to determine whether you have endogenous depression (often linked to genetics) or situational or reactive depression. Depending on your diagnosis and unique body chemistry, you may have to trial more than one or two medications to find one that's right for you.

If you are taking a medication to affect your mood or creativity, consult with a psychiatrist—not just any medical doctor—to work through any challenges you might experience in taking more than one drug. Don't change any dosages without speaking to a psychiatrist. And always check for any side effects or contraindications.

Always be open with your doctor or doctors about how a particular medication is affecting you and whether you're using it as directed or skipping doses, using more than was prescribed, or combining it with other medications or with mood-altering substances including recreational "street drugs" (which aren't necessarily sold on the street—many people purchase them through dark-web online ordering). Never stop taking medications abruptly: discuss getting off them with a psychiatrist before making your decision, and be sure you taper off under medical supervision. If you're seeing a therapist, make sure they know about your medications.

If you're not taking a comprehensive approach to medication, if you're getting prescriptions from more than one doctor and not talking to anyone about how they might interact with each other, you're not getting the best medical care. Be up front with the medical professionals you work with. Otherwise, you run the risk of becoming overmedicated or mixing two drugs—recreational or pharmaceutical—that should not be used together.

Many people are curious about psychedelics and intrigued by anecdotal stories about how they have been useful for addressing a variety of problems. Preliminary research on the use of psychedelics to treat addiction, depression, PTSD, and end-of-life anxiety is promising, but the studies on these topics have involved careful preparation and support as well as very controlled environments. It's not safe to assume that without those elements, someone's experience of psychedelics will yield similar results. Only the psychedelic drug ketamine has been granted FDA approval. Using psychedelics in anything other than a research setting supervised by a physician and licensed psychotherapists may put you in complicated mind terrain and, for some people, could lead to danger.

Once many years ago, I got a call in the middle of the night from a client who had decided to try a psychedelic. She was taking an SSRI and didn't realize that the ego dissolution that she experienced, which is common with psychedelics, was a symbolic death not an actual one. Fearing she was dying, she called 911. After being stabilized, she was charged with possession and thrown in jail, and I was the only person she felt comfortable calling to get released. I felt terrible that she had gotten herself into so much trouble.

If you're considering a psychedelic experience, research the topic and develop a solid knowledge base of how these substances interact with the mind, brain, and nervous system. Also, look closely at your history (including your family history) and your current degree of stability in your personal life and self as well as the potential danger of having the psychedelic experience if you are on medications of any type. And then, again, only use them in a research setting (after researching clinical trials online and being accepted into a legitimate research study supervised by a physician and licensed psychotherapists).

Anecdotal reports, reported in the press, seem to show that a dose of San Pedro, ibogaine (derived from an African plant that has psychedelic qualities), ayahuasca, or LSD is so transformative that you never again return to addiction or depression. There are cases of people who suffered with severe mental and emotional afflictions obtaining great benefits from undergoing treatment through a psychedelic journey experience. Some have reported having experienced a feeling of oneness and sacred awe as a result, awakening a spiritual outlook that freed them from their trauma, addictions, and/or depressive disorders. According to the American Addiction Centers website, "Treatment for several addictive substances with ibogaine results in a 20–50 percent rate of abstinence at a one-year follow-up point, on average, and that includes people working to end opioid addiction. Comparatively, Suboxone treatment for opioid addiction shows an 8.6 percent success rate once the person no longer needs to take Suboxone."[8] Recently, research showed that MDMA (also known as the street drug "Molly" or "Ecstasy") can be effective for PTSD, and psilocybin (the main ingredient in psychedelic mushrooms) is effective for treating depression.[9] I suspect that given the money being poured into research on psychedelics, we'll have a lot more information to work from in the coming years—including on safe dosages. It's long overdue.

I'm fascinated by the potential of psychedelics in part because I witnessed some of the history of research into these substances. Early research into the benefits of psychedelics looked promising but was shut down at Harvard University in the 1960s. Soon after that, some psychiatrists began a project at the Maryland Psychiatric Research Center in Baltimore that spanned a research patient population of alcoholics, drug addicts, schizophrenics, cancer patients, terminally ill patients, and eventually clergy and creative artists as well. I was a young intern working in the music therapy department of the project under music therapist Helen Bonny, author of *Music and Your Mind* (1990). I was able to witness observing psychiatrist Dr. Stanislav Grof, as well as Dr. William Richards, Dr. Joan Halifax-Roshi, and other research assistants, providing LSD-assisted therapy. Many of the patient participants underwent deeply psychological forays into the reexperiencing of their own birth trauma and reported having a profound and ineffable mystical and spiritually transformative experience. So, with this background and area of expertise, I understand the current day interest in psychedelic exploration and research.

However, we don't know how many people who undergo psychedelic trips or shamanic journeys facilitated by ayahuasca or psychedelic mushrooms never again need medication or therapy. What we do know is that like anyone, people who have had transformative experiences due to psychedelics will likely experience grief, anxiety, depression, anger—a range of normal human emotions—afterward. Are they prepared to handle them if they have often self-medicated their emotions in the past?

Also, let me reiterate: If you want to use psychedelics, do it as part of a research study. You'll be supervised by a physician and often—for example, with the MAPS project (MAPS stand for Multidisciplinary Association for Psychedelic Studies)—with two psychotherapists, who are trained to support you through any unpleasant and frightening experiences you have. Otherwise, your quest for healing might result in a traumatic journey (what is commonly referred to as a "bad trip"). We don't know why so many people undergoing psychedelic experiences have mystical, pleasurable, and psychologically insightful trips while others have a most uncomfortable and sometimes painful experience.

THE SPIRITUAL PIECE AND
THE ALLURE OF ONE BIG FIX

Some people choose to journey using psychedelics because they view it as a spiritual practice: to feel their connection to the sacred and strengthen their relationship to it, whether they think of the sacred as God or Spirit, universal consciousness, the human spirit, a higher power, or something else. It's true that spiritual practices can help you experience deep feelings of relaxation and inner calm as well as less tension and anxiety. You might even feel a sense of sacredness and oneness with creation. The former Harvard professor of psychology, author, and spiritual teacher Ram Dass told me a story that sums up my beliefs about how to have a profound spiritual experience. The Indian saint, guru, and sage Maharaji Neem Karolyi Baba, when given a large dose of LSD (2,000 micrograms) by Ram Dass, told him, "These medicines were used in Kullu Valley long ago. But yogis have lost that knowledge. They were used with fasting. Nobody knows now. To take them with no effect, your mind must be firmly fixed on God." Maharaji Ram Dass told me that Maharaji Neem Karolyi Baba acted odd and withdrawn for several hours, and when he came down, he turned to Ram Dass and said in essence that the drug seemed useful but that it was better to learn how to become the Divine rather than rely exclusively on visiting God briefly and then having to leave.[10]

There are spiritual practices that might generate the same effects as a journey without any of the risks. Your spiritual practices might include meditation, reading from spiritual texts, chanting and singing sacred sounds known as mantras, doing Bhakti yoga (often combined with chanting or singing), or something else. Mystics have said that such practices offer greater happiness and even bliss, as well as a sense of connection to all that is loving within you and outside of you. Common long-term results of spiritual practice include cultivating compassion, gratitude, kindness, and a sense of awe and wonder. All of these pay-offs have value themselves as well as making it easier to embrace your creativity and expand upon it.

When you use spiritual practices, and especially mindfulness, paying attention to something simple such as the breath or the feeling of being in a yoga pose and holding it, they can become portals to your unconscious mind and collective unconscious shared by all, as well as your inner creative resources. Mindfulness is a direct conduit to the rich inner world of dreams, memories, and fantasies, unlocking the door to endless imagination. It relaxes the conscious mind, bringing the creative unconscious online.

I'll add that regardless of how profound and intense an experience you have using high-dose psychedelics, if you find days, months, or even a year afterward you are not doing well, there is no shame in going back on a medication that you were taking before if it will help you feel well and whole again. Don't let the allure of "one big fix" blind you to what you as a unique person need to function optimally.

MICRODOSING, CREATIVITY, AND MOOD

Microdosing is the daily ingestion of tiny doses of psychedelic sub-stances such as psilocybin mushrooms, LSD-25, ketamine, DMT, and MDA, typically for a limited period such as thirty, fifty, or ninety days. Some people say that taking a microdose of one-tenth or even one-twentieth of a psychedelic can enhance creativity and/or modulate mental health disorders such as anxiety, depression, addiction, and

PTSD, but the research isn't there yet to rule out the possibility that what they're experiencing is merely placebo effect.

Psychologist James Fadiman, a former undergraduate student of Ram Dass's while at Harvard, was a pioneer in early psychedelic research and today is a proponent of microdosing. He reports that over two thousand people have contacted him through his website (microdosing psychedelics.com) to report that their experience of microdosing was very positive. Many people who say they have been struggling with PTSD, traumatic brain injury, and treatment-resistant depression have reported to him that they are doing very well after microdosing. In fact, many claim they have been able to discontinue mainstream medications and remain off of them after just a brief period of microdosing. In my psychotherapy practice, I haven't seen any of my patients or clients who microdose report negative experiences. Like those reporting their results to Fadiman, they are seeing positive results: They tell me it has enhanced their life, work, and relationships and boosted their creativity. One client, a young lead guitarist, says her finger dexterity has improved along with her versatility and work ethic, which has reduced some of the draining emotional conflicts in her band. But is it the microdosing or is it placebo effect that is giving her that perception? I hope that someday we'll know more.

Remember, it is likely illegal to use psychedelics in *any* amount where you live. You can get fired from a job if you're discovered to have used illegal substances such as marijuana or microdoses of psilocybin. You can end up with a felony on your record. Driving under the influence of illegal drugs and many legal ones is dangerous even if you are under the legal limits of, say, alcohol. The patchwork legalization and decriminalization of cannabis is a good example of how the medical and legal communities can be slow in recognizing the medical value of substances that have been illegal and understanding what is risky and what isn't. Partner with your doctor before deciding what medications and substances to take, and be aware of your vulnerabilities given the laws where you are. I think that within the next ten years, we will have enough research on psychedelics that they will be brought into mainstream medical and psychiatric uses. For now, however, if medication is needed, my advice is to rely on ones that have been extensively researched and approved by the FDA.

For enhanced creativity, I recommend a daily mindfulness practice combined with adopting the mind-sets and habits of highly creative people. Michael Murphy, the co-founder of the Esalen Institute in Big Sur, California, and award-winning journalist and author George Leonard, along with the prolific transpersonal psychologist Ken Wilber, co-created Integral Transformative Practice™, an approach to mind-body-spirit wellness that emphasizes healing in stages. Like me, Murphy and Leonard believe that over time, using gentle interventions systemically will create a reliable outcome of improved wellness—at least, for most people.

MORE WAYS TO STAY HEALTHY PHYSICALLY AND MENTALLY

Regardless of what your mental health or psychological conditions are, the better your health habits are, the easier it will be to maximize your creativity and reduce the volatility in your moods, activity level, and ability to focus. Clean up your diet with the help of a nutritionist, paying close attention to how sugar, processed foods, alcohol, and caffeine affect you. Journaling about your symptoms and meditating with the intention of gaining insights about your diet can help you alter your eating patterns to promote better self-regulation.

Develop some new behavioral practices such as creating lists to keep yourself focused, not giving yourself too many choices so as to avoid becoming overwhelmed, and mindfully listening when others are talking to avoid speaking too quickly. An ADHD coach can help you identify new habits you can start developing to take greater control over your ADHD symptoms.

Keep in mind that exercise can be a powerful tool for boosting creativity, according to several studies.[11] It can also help you manage your moods as well as offering other benefits. Former journalist and *Runners World* editor Scott Douglas, author of *Running Is My Therapy* (2018), has written that he had suffered from chronic depression since middle school, managing it through running.[12] Many studies have shown the benefits of exercise on mental health, including the one mentioned earlier that was done by a team led by Bessel van der Kolk, author of *The Body Keeps the Score* (2014), and have found yoga can be effective for treating PTSD symptoms, helping people better the physical discomfort of their fear response and increase their self-awareness.[13] And those who exercise regularly may be less likely in the future to become depressed. How much you exercise is up to you, but I recommend that you do at least the minimum amount recommended by the CDC: 150 minutes a week of aerobic exercise and two days a week of weight training that works all your muscle groups.

Remember, too, that nature has many benefits for mood. Getting enough vitamin D from sunlight will help you maintain more positive mood states (it also makes it easier to sustain a healthy immune system), and cortisol levels drop within minutes when you're in a natural setting.

Mental and physical health support each other. Don't underestimate your need to address both so you feel better, are more focused, alert, and energized, and are better able to access your creativity.

TREATING ADDICTION

In working with clients in the entertainment industry, I have experienced up close and firsthand the anguish and profound suffering of many talented people who have self-medicated with alcohol and drugs as a result of untreated depression, bipolar disorder, or anxiety. I've watched with an equal mix of horror and compassion when some of my artistic patients descended into the hell of addictions in their attempts to self-medicate for these disorders. I have driven a patient to a rehabilitation center while his nose was bleeding all over his bright white shirt while he screamed at me, "I am not using cocaine!" I have also experienced the great joy of visiting patients several weeks or even months into treatment and seeing the profound transformation that followed from their detoxifying, getting clean of the addiction, learning about new treatment methods such as Somatic Experiencing, equine therapy, eye movement desensitization and reprocessing (EMDR), yoga, and mindfulness-based therapies. Elisha Goldstein and I wrote the chapter "Mindfulness, Trauma, and Trance: A Mindfulness-Based Psychotherapeutic Approach" in Ellen Langer's *The Wiley Blackwell Handbook of Mindfulness and Psychotherapy,* vol. 2 (2014), because we have experienced the power of such therapies in treating addiction, among other psychological issues.[14] That said, for many people, getting the right psychotropic medicines to bring balance and harmony to the brain is a key component to sobriety, too. And as I mentioned earlier, a nutritional evaluation that can shed light on deficits you can address might help you maintain positive moods and make a big difference in your ability to stay sober.

Self-medication is a part of the human experience, but nowadays, when I'm invited backstage to concerts by classic rock musicians and singer/songwriters, it's rare for me to see as much as a bottle of beer. That's because many artists have discovered that the quality of their creative output is far higher when they're not self-medicating with alcohol and drugs. One musician told me that in the past she had been flying wild and high while writing and playing music, but now that she's no longer using drugs, when she writes, she feels she is playing or dancing with a pure energy that feels organic, expansive, and joyful—and pure creative energy that comes directly from her soul and brings her bliss.

If you have any history of drug or alcohol addiction, or any family history of them, it's essential to work with a professional psychiatrist and a therapist who are familiar with addictions as well as medications for treating them. They can carefully assist you in avoiding the rabbit hole of ongoing substance abuse. Through the practice of mindfulness and meditation, you can support yourself in bringing harmony and equanimity to your mind and body. Add to that a healthy diet, exercise, and, if needed, frequent attendance at twelve-step meetings as well as medications prescribed by a psychiatrist, and it will be far easier for you to live a creative life than if you're trying to manage it all on your own with no help and limited tools.

One of the reasons people who could benefit from twelve-step meetings are reluctant to attend is because the spiritual language puts them off, but addiction treatment that integrates a spiritual outlook has worked for many, even those who aren't traditionally religious. For some, the higher power you surrender to might be the power of the human spirit or the twelve-step community's collective wisdom and motivation.

In fact, the origin of a spiritual angle to Alcoholics Anonymous (AA) might surprise you. Bill W., one of the founders of AA, wrote to psychologist Carl Jung in 1961 to express his gratitude for his advising of a patient named Rowland H., who had come to Jung for help with his alcohol addiction. Bill W. pointed out that Jung's forthright admission that he believed the medical and psychological communities could no longer help Rowland H. earned the patient's trust. Bill W. wrote that Jung's advice to the man was to aim to "become the subject of a spiritual or religious experience—in short, a genuine conversion." He added, "You pointed out how such an experience, if brought about, might remotivate him when nothing else could." Jung's honest and compassionate response to the man, Bill W. said, "was beyond doubt the first foundation stone upon which our Society [Alcoholics Anonymous] has since been built."[15] Jung, known for his work with the unconscious, was not promoting a particular religion or theology. He was talking about a shift in perspective that comes from a mystical experience. That's something that can be experienced within or outside of a religion (and outside of a psychedelic experience).

Jung was known to disdain group therapy, believing it inferior to personal work toward individuation (healing in the form of reclaiming aspects of the self that a person had denied out of shame or fear). However, his student, Margarita Luttichau, had written to Bill W. in 1947 after she and Jung had attended an analytical society conference in Switzerland and talked about their experiences. She told him that Jung "gave me extraordinarily complete instructions how it [healing within a group model] might be managed."[16] The support of a twelve-step group might be key to your managing your addiction.

And while we're on the topic, be aware that you can become dependent on or even addicted to mood-altering medications, which is why I strongly emphasize tapering off them under medical supervision if you and your medical team decide that's something to try. I especially caution you about a class of anti-anxiety medications call benzodiazepenes, which are only for acute episodes (panic attacks, for example) and should be discontinued after two weeks to prevent significant side effects and dependence. If a client of mine is prescribed this drug in the emergency room, I say that's fine, but you need to come in as soon as possible to discuss what happened, and we need to get you to a psychiatrist who can review your medications list (if the client has one) and adjust it. I know the client might need to take an anti-anxiety medication that is safe for long-term use. Stevie Nicks from the band Fleetwood Mac has spoken of her own struggle with a benzodiazepene called Klonopin, saying she believes it led to extreme weight gain and a severe dampening of her creativity for years after it was prescribed for her post-rehab for cocaine addiction. The prescribing psychiatrist kept her on this benzodiazepene, a most costly decision.[17]

Here's the bottom line: weaving new neural networks for healthier and more productive ways of dealing with problematic moods and mental habits lays the foundation for personal transformation that can be dramatic. And research now shows that the brain is far more plastic than we once thought. As the saying, coined by neuropsychologist Donald Hebb, goes, "neurons that fire together wire together": the more often a neural pathway in the brain is used, the more it's reinforced and the stronger it becomes. Your brain's gray matter actually thickens in some areas as you practice new thoughts or habits. You can become less aggressive and more assertive, and you start to express qualities you didn't know you could possess.

So, if you have a mental health condition, regardless of how mild you think it is, I hope you'll let go of any outdated ideas about medication, creativity, and ways to gain a greater sense of tranquility, motivation, and wellness. Remember: you are a unique individual whose path may differ from that of others. Don't let the shame of stigmatization hold you back from making changes that will give you the foundation for improved health and well-being as well as greater creativity.

Chapter Nine

Mindful Decision Making

Once, a CEO had a big decision to make. Should he go ahead with a proposed merger? He was feeling pressured to say yes and had heard that going for a walk in the woods to clear his head would facilitate making better decisions by putting him in touch with his intuition. Determined to get an answer that day, he went into the woods and came out a short time later having made the decision to agree to the deal. It turned out to be an extraordinarily terrible decision, and his company lost millions.

A few years later, in a private conversation over lunch, I asked the CEO about his decision-making process. He told me that for most of his professional life, he had relied on his creative instincts, but when faced with this big decision, feeling pressed for time, he went with his head, abandoning his gut feeling that the merger wouldn't work out. During that walk in the woods, he said, his inner voice had been screaming at him, but then his head reminded him that the merger looked great on paper. What's more, he had been afraid that his company would miss out on a big opportunity if he walked away from the deal. He expressed that had he only found mindfulness meditation earlier, he probably would have sought inner counsel as well as coaching to help him slow down the pace of decision making. He felt that might have averted the disaster.

Timothy Leary, counterculture figure and former psychology professor at Harvard University, famously said, "Turn on, tune in, drop out," meaning that to raise consciousness, people should use hallucinogenics, tune in to their inner wisdom and creativity, and free themselves of the constrictions of society to forge a new path. My spin on his advice for those wanting to make good decisions is let go, tune in, and move forward: let go of your fears, tune in to your inner wisdom through the practice of mindfulness meditation, and move forward into action—that is, enter a decision-making process that is guided by your inner wisdom.

LET GO OF YOUR FEARS AS YOU FACE YOUR DECISION

There will always be risk in decision making, but making decisions is necessary for transformation, and you can relate to the uncertainty about the consequences of your various options differently.

One of the most common fears about decision making is a fear of running out of time and resources. Highly creative people and people who meditate have different perceptions of time, recognizing that time spent in total absorption, staring at a blank canvas or observing nature, is not wasted. They recognize that these are forms of meditation that can serve as a portal into open mind and core creativity. The more a person practices absorption, the easier it will be for them to enter into an open state very quickly, accessing intuition and core creativity that can help in decision making.

When you are up against a deadline and funds are limited, the fear of those limitations will make it difficult to access all your resources as you face your decision. Observe the language you use when thinking about your deadline—is it a "killer" or "drop-dead" *dead*line that has you "under the gun"? How do those terms make you feel compared to "due date" or "completion date"? What will the actual consequences be if you are late? Could you move the due date? The language you use about decision making can influence your perceptions and make you unnecessarily anxious.

As you think about your financial limitations, are you considering that you might be able to attain more money or use it more effectively by accessing your creativity? When you're thinking you might "go broke"—as if your ability to tap into financial resources could irretrievably shatter—reframe your situation. You can have strong reasons for sticking to a budget and not creating delays that would be costly, without creating anxiety that shuts down your creative processes.

In the last chapter, I talked about relating to time and money differently and using creativity to find new sources for them. When you're making a decision, you can ask someone to help you clear space to focus on the process by removing some of your distractions. You might hire people to do what you could do yourself but don't have the time for when you're facing the need to make a decision sooner rather than later. These actions can help you let go of your fears because they'll open your eyes to more options available to you.

Also, while sometimes you might be very much aware of your fear and any pressures you are under, at other times, you might not recognize the extent to which you're operating under duress. Fear and stress, along with anger and grief, are likely to block you from a state of open mind. When that happens, what comes up for you during a walk in nature or when meditating might not be clarity and creative ideas but confusion, hesitancy, and ambivalence. Even if your fear isn't manifesting as a sensation or emotion, don't ignore the sense that something is wrong with the decision you're leaning toward, like the CEO did. Meditate on it rather than expecting the woods to solve your problem within an hour.

Most of us want to escape the discomfort of being in uncertainty, so we're tempted to make a quick decision we later regret. However, if we fear making a wrong decision, we also might procrastinate, letting the decision somehow get made for us and then we have to live with the consequences. Or, we may let an opportunity pass us by. If we give in to our fears and rush our process or procrastinate, we shut down our core creativity, intuition, and inner wisdom. If we resist observing problems and assessing what to do about them, we might not be able to salvage a situation by the time we take a look at it. And attachment to an unrealistic goal of making a decision that will absolutely result in a specific outcome creates a lot of suffering. We have to be willing to accept some uncertainty about the results of our decisions.

As the Taoist proverb goes, the slower you go, the faster you'll move toward enlightened, mindful awareness. In making decisions, the challenge is to pace yourself, releasing the fears of your frustrated, demanding self that demands to know right away what your decision will be and feel sure it's the "right" one. Richer possibilities and better outcomes result from engaging fully in a nonlinear, creative process of mindful decision making. Anxiety and fear are signals that it's time for you to gently apply the brakes, releasing your fear so you can tolerate the uncertainty that's a normal part of decision making. In slowing down, you are actually laying the foundation for a more solid future with your project or organization or relationships with significant others and coworkers.

To make better decisions, start changing your mind-set about uncertainty so it's not so frightening that it shuts you down. Your decision might lead to a failure, but it also might lead to a success. Why focus on one over the other? If you let go of your fear of being devastated by a failure, it will be easier to experience equanimity as you weigh your options. Remember, highly creative people don't automatically resist transition, uncertainty, or "mis-takes"; they often embrace them enthusiastically. Mindfulness practice helps you develop this mind-set of looking at possibilities with excitement and optimism instead of fear and pessimism. If you end up being unhappy with the outcome of your choice, with the result of your "mis-take," you can mindfully observe that and say to yourself, "This is not where I want to be right now" and make a new choice. There's an old shamanic saying that when you have a choice to go right or left, it's best to go left and cross over on the bridge of the river of time. It means that when making big life decisions, we shouldn't be afraid to embark on a radically new path. That's easier to do when you stop fearing mistakes and start using them to get closer to a desired outcome through a different route. Persevere! Your response to evidence that you have failed can be this: "Let's not fix that quite yet. Let's explore it and its potential."

Practicing mindfulness fosters a possibility mind-set. When you're mindfully creative and appreciating the flow state as you craft and shape ideas, your emotions are tempered. It becomes easier to see setbacks as potential turning points in a continual process of creativity. You develop a more holistic view of problems, seeing their complexities but also the multiple possibilities for solutions and ways to deal with unexpectedly unpleasant outcomes.

As you develop your mindfulness practice, it will be easier to feel a sense of spaciousness and less pressure as you consider your decision. Let's face it: decisions can feel weighty. The first time Neil Armstrong walked on the Moon, the world was mesmerized by how he was able to easily and fluidly bounce along its cratered surface, unencumbered by the strong gravity of Earth. We all seek to free ourselves of the weighty burdens that make us anxious, pessimist, cynical, and unable to fully trust ourselves as we make decisions. By accessing open mind, you enter a gravity-free zone where the weight of any decision is alleviated. There's an old saying: "If you have only thirty minutes to meditate, meditate for thirty minutes. If you only have five minutes to meditate, meditate for an hour." If you don't slow down your decision making, your perception is likely to become distorted by your sense of urgency and pressure.

Creative people get into the flow and lose track of time, but creative people who meditate become extremely efficient at using the time they have, shrinking or expanding it. Of course, that doesn't actually happen—if only we had that magical power! What does happen is that fears about running out of time fade, making it easier for you to relax into a receptive, absorbing state where ideas and insights come to you as a result of intuition and core creativity. Taking a mindful pause and doing a body scan (like you would do when using the Body Observation Meditation) to release the energy of fear can help. Then, take the time to work with a portal into open mind and refresh yourself on the creative habits that can strengthen your creative abilities. Get curious and look from many angles at the challenges you're facing.

And then check in with your intuition.

TUNE IN WITHIN

If you feel you can't take the time to sit with your decision, is it because you feel you don't have the time to do that? Whenever I hear someone say, "I don't have the time," I always say, "Well, if you don't have the time, then you'll miss the deeper inner rhyme." It's my gentle reminder that they need to slow down and go within, entering a state of open mind. That's especially important when in the process of making a big decision.

There is a power in not knowing and not needing to know and a power in not doing and not needing to do—that's my philosophy, influenced by the work of Milton Erickson. He observed that when you tell someone they don't need to think about making a decision yet, you invite the unconscious to speak its truth and wisdom—and you invite them to release the weighty burden of a decision with unknown consequences.[1]

Even if it's your mentor or a very trusted colleague telling you "Here's what I would do if I were in your situation," tune in within and listen to your intuition. You don't want someone else making the decision for you or unduly influencing you. I knew this intellectually but ignored my own advice, dismissing my intuition, to my detriment, back in 2008 when I dreamed about the stock market crashing. Remember, you want people on your council and in your pod to give you insights based on their knowledge and experience, but also to be active and challenge you to think more creatively and be more open to new ideas. Their role is not to tell you what to do. Listen to their counsel, but then continue with a decision-making process that includes intuitive wisdom.

Over time, as you come to fully own your creativity as a powerful asset, you'll be more resilient, optimistic that you can extricate yourself from the worst situations and emerge into better ones. You'll find you're not panicking or despairing when change is forced upon you and instead entering a mindful, creative decision-making process.

Slowing down as part of a mindfulness practice to get into open mind and tune in to your creativity and intuition can help you see when you're falling into old patterns. You don't want to be automatically choosing to please other people or abdicate to someone you think is wiser than you, ignoring your values and priorities. You want to tune in to yourself to make a more conscious decision, one that feels—and is—right for you. When Facebook offered Evan Spiegel of Snap, Inc., the parent company of Snapchat, $3 billion for the company he had created, he refused the offer because he felt he wanted to continue to invest in this creative project. Some said he was crazy because social media networks were known to sometimes lose their popularity and financial value very quickly, but today, Snapchat is valued at over $100 billion.[2] Spiegel's courage to stick with his inner vision to continue creatively shaping the company, taking the risk of walking away from $3 billion, is echoed by people who access their core creativity and intuition and sense when it is right to stay with what they are doing and continue with it even if it involves risk.

Similarly, in the early 1980s, singer/songwriter/musician Neil Young was sued by his record company because David Geffen, the head of Geffen Records, decided that two albums of his in a row weren't commercial enough. Ultimately, David Geffen backed off from the lawsuit and apologized.[3] To Young, money wasn't as important as artistic freedom.

Going within and accessing your intuition can help you find the courage to be true to your values and convictions. If you consult someone who offers their own intuitive wisdom to you, and it aligns with what you know within, it can be even easier to claim what you know deep down and use it to guide you in making your choices, as my client Elaine learned.

ELAINE AND A DECISION INFORMED BY VALUES AND INTUITION

A psychoanalyst in the Midwest once referred to me a wealthy woman named Elaine who, after a year of therapy, was still struggling with a major decision: Should she leave her marriage or end the affair she was having? She loved her husband and felt guilty about cheating on him. She was a mother and didn't want to break up her family. Her choice might seem to be an easy one, but Elaine couldn't seem to make it. Additionally, she wanted to know why she was violating her deepest held values. It would turn out that intuition was the key not only to making her decision but to releasing some old emotions from a past trauma she hadn't fully processed that were causing her to act out of sync with her heart's longings.

When Elaine showed up in my office in a conservative business suit and high heels, I had to wonder what she thought as she made her way through my Zen garden to my home office door. I could see she had obeyed the sign that said, "Please remove your shoes before entering" because she stood awkwardly in my doorway, shoes in one hand, boxy briefcase in another, as I welcomed her and motioned for her to sit down on my couch. When she did, she placed her briefcase on her lap and carefully balanced her shoes on top of it.

Her eyes darted toward my statues of the Buddha and my posters of a Tibetan monastery and the view from Esalen in Big Sur. As I introduced myself, I admit I was thinking that the contrast between the two of us couldn't have been greater. I wasn't surprised when she quickly offered to pay for the three-hour session and end it early. She said, "My therapist told me your California-type techniques could help me, but I don't see how. It's been a year and I'm still stuck."

"Why don't we at least give it a try?" I said. "And thank you for taking off your shoes. You can keep them safe on that mat next to you while we explore some of your feelings about me and coming to this space, which I'm sure is very different from your psychotherapist's office."

"I'd say," she said under her breath.

"I guess this office wasn't quite what you expected."

She placed her briefcase by the side of the couch, and then she leaned back and took a deep breath—a good sign that she was relaxing. I asked her to tell me why she was in my office and listened attentively as she told me her story. When she finished, I said, "Would you be willing to take a risk and jump right in and do a real California-type therapy thing? It's very easy."

I told her we were just going to close our eyes at the same time and each of us explore our inner world and our inner bodies. She said, "I'm not quite sure what you mean by inner world, but in my work"—she had told me she had a high-pressure job running a business—"I'll often close my eyes before I make a big decision to tune in to what my body's telling me."

"Yes! That's exactly what I mean. I want you to explore your intuition through your body's somatic sense of self. You're free to share anything that's coming to you, and I'll share with you anything that I'm intuitively seeing, hearing, or feeling."

Both of us closed our eyes.

We were quiet for about twenty minutes before I opened my eyes and broke the silence.

"I have to ask you about a couple of images that have come to me—more than once. It doesn't mean anything to me but maybe it does to you."

I described seeing a young woman in the moonlight, running along a road somewhere in the woods, clearly frantic, and the same young woman standing outside of a funeral home.

Immediately, Elaine's formal demeanor disappeared, and she began to cry. "I can't believe what you're saying—I hadn't thought about that for years. Since I was a kid." She explained that as a teenager, she and her friend had been driving at night in her family's car, without having received permission. Elaine was behind the wheel when a deer jumped out in front of them, causing them to crash and her passenger to be seriously injured. Elaine had run to get help, but by the time it arrived, it was too late. Her friend had succumbed to her injuries. Elaine's mother told her not to go to the funeral, not to communicate with her friend's deeply distraught family, and not to ever speak of the accident again— best to move on, she was told. Soon afterward, her family moved away from the area, and Elaine grew up, married, began her career, and kept the memory repressed for decades.

For the next hour or so, she sobbed on my couch, releasing her grief, and by the end of the three-hour session, she had clarity about her marriage and why she had cheated on her husband. She understood that on some level, she didn't feel entitled to the happiness she had at home and was unconsciously sabotaging it. Recognizing that, she was certain about what she was going to do and determined to do it. She would end the affair and recommit herself to her marriage. I had to credit intuition for her breakthrough.

My own experience and my clinical and coaching experience has taught me time and time again the value of slowing everything down and listening to the body's wisdom as well as your intuition, which should play a key role in your decision making because it comes from a deeper sense of knowing that goes beyond the limits of the rational mind.

NOT JUST INTUITION

As described earlier, I will sometimes go to sleep at night intending to have a dream that offers me insights. Sometimes, however, your intuition will create a dream so vivid and memorable that you strongly sense it has an important message for you. That happened back when I was a young man finishing up my undergraduate studies in Amherst, Massachusetts, trying to decide between attending graduate school on the East or West Coast.

I had visited California a few times, done a little research on it, and brought my plan for possibly moving there to members of my Wisdom Council of Support to get their feedback. Fortunately, no one was completely negative about my decision, but I still wasn't sure. It was a big commitment for me. Then, one night, I had a dream in which I was sitting in the driver's seat of a covered wagon, having crossed the Rocky Mountains, my girlfriend at my side. We were at the top of the Sierra Nevada range and looking toward San Francisco. I turned to my girlfriend, pointed straight ahead, and said to her, "There's gold in them hills." When I awoke from this dream, I sat up and wrote it down. As I did, I had the sense that this gold rush image included a covered wagon because my unconscious was telling me, "We've got you covered, so go ahead and strike it rich out on this new frontier." I wrote, "I will find my gold on the West Coast."

However, I had laid the groundwork for this intuitive message by letting go of my fear of uncertainty, acknowledging my resources of time and money might be greater than it seemed at first glance, and tuning in by meditating and paying attention to my dreams. Only then did I take action.

Sometimes, "intuitive" messages are not what they seem—they're rooted in fear rather than genuine intuition. If you feel a strong sense of urgency to move forward right now while also feeling anxious and not having done any research to support your decision, it's a sign that you should question whether you're mistaking fear for intuitive wisdom. Continue to meditate, seeking insights about the ideas that you're entertaining. Consider cueing yourself at night to have an intuitive dream and using the Gestalt Inquiry Technique you learned about in chapter 5, "Absorbing Creative Stimulation and Getting into Open Mind Consciousness," to better understand its messages (or simply use the technique to learn from your logical, feeling, and wise "selves," as described in the exercise).

MOVE FORWARD INTO BETTER DECISION MAKING

While slowing down will reduce your sense of urgency and alleviate the weight and pressure of a decision, you will also have to move forward into exploring your thoughts about your decision-making process and any hidden beliefs about your competence and ability to make a good one. You can start taking this action before you slow down and tune in to your core internal resources, but it's important not to skip that step. And once you do, you may still need to look closely at your options and make some choices to act on.

You'll have to make many decisions as you move forward into living a more creative life in sync with your deepest desires. If you feel overwhelmed, it may be that your fear of making a "wrong" decision or missing an opportunity by taking time with your decision-making process is creating a sort of amnesia about your successful decision making in the past. By now, you know that even an outcome you didn't like at first may have become a stepping-stone to experiences that you're glad you had, so those past "bad" decisions aren't so bad after all if you look at their upsides.

I suggest you try the following exercise with a decision that you've thought of as a "bad" one because you didn't like the initial outcome, and then do it again with a decision that resulted in a neutral or positive outcome to see what you learn from your own decision making.

EXERCISE: JOURNALING TO LEARN FROM A PAST DECISION

Take out a journal to do this exercise, recording your answers to the questions.

When making the past decision, did you ask yourself these four questions: *Why? Why not? Why not now? If not now, then when?* If you did, were they helpful in bringing out a desirable outcome? How?

If you didn't ask yourself the four questions, identify what your answers to them might have been. Take the time to answer each one as if you were in that past moment, considering the decision before you.

As you look at the answers you wrote then, or now in retrospect, try to identify ways in which asking the four questions might be helpful when making decisions going forward. For example, you might want to consider whether asking the four questions, or not asking them, helped you achieve a desirable outcome or could have helped you achieve a better outcome. Let's say your answer to the question "Why not now?" would have been "Because I am not sure I'm emotionally ready for a new relationship." You now have more information about your decision-making process that you can learn from. You might realize that in the past, you had not been in touch with your feelings about a decision and that in the future, you would benefit from being in touch with them as you make decisions. Suppose your answer to "Why not now?" was "No reason other than my wish for total certainty about the outcome, which isn't possible anyway," and you went ahead and made the decision and dealt with anything unpleasant about the outcome without regretting your choice. From this answer, you can learn that it's important to ask yourself, "Why not now?" and accept that no outcome is 100 percent certain.

Now, answer these questions:

As you consider your past decision, how did you feel about the process and the outcome?

What did you think when making your decision?

What did you do when making your decision? For example, what steps did you take?

Did you receive one or more intuitive messages regarding your decision, and, if so, what were they? Did you follow them? Why or why not?

Did you meditate during your decision-making process?

If you meditated, what type of meditation did you do and why?

Did you consider doing a body scan meditation to get in touch with any sensations that could help you be more certain of how you felt about a potential decision?

If you did a body scan meditation, what did you learn? And if you didn't, would you be willing to try using one the next time you make a decision?

Looking back on the role of meditating or not meditating while undergoing your decision-making process, what if any insights do you have about the value of meditation for you?

What have you learned about your decision making in the past that can help you in your decision making now and in the future?

Once you've analyzed your decision-making process and its outcome for decisions that led to both undesirable and desirable (or neutral) outcomes, you might want to do the Return to the Scene to Change It Visualization from chapter 3, returning to a scene of you wrestling with a big decision. As you do that meditation, allow yourself to feel any discomfort regarding the uncertainty. As described in the instructions for the exercise, pay attention to what you heard, who was saying it, and what you felt and thought. Then, change the scene so that the decision-making process leads to a better outcome. When you end your meditation, observe how you feel. What did you imagine yourself doing differently?

You might also want to go back to chapter 5, "Absorbing Creative Stimulation and Getting into Open Mind Consciousness," and use the gestalt technique exercise for asking your logical, feeling, and wise selves for their input about a decision you're facing. You could even embody the decision to learn what it has to tell you about itself.

More understanding of your past decision-making processes can help you in the future, so don't beat yourself up for having had imperfect processes that led to an unpleasant outcome. You can't change the past, but you can change how you frame it and how you will make decisions in the future.

MAKING A DECISION USING YOUR ANALYTICAL, INTUITIVE, AND CREATIVE ABILITIES

Now that you've learned more about your own past decision-making process, I'd like to expand upon the strategies for making good decisions, putting together your many resources for guiding you in making decisions going forward.

Your logical, analytical self can weigh the pros and cons of your choices (more on that shortly), while your intuitive self may get messages that are visual, somatic, or auditory. For example, you might feel a heaviness near your chest and a sense of being resigned or helpless as you think about one of your options, or you feel a sense of excitement and enthusiasm. You might keep hearing certain words in your head as you think about your decision. You also might feel a surge of energy as you think about the choice you want to make or feel a sense of dread or apprehension that causes you to feel you have low energy. Finally, you might find you can't stop thinking about what you want to do, no matter how much you try to talk yourself out of it.

You might also have an inner knowing that something is wrong—while not feeling any emotion or sensation to back that up. In his book *Cosmic Religion,* Albert Einstein wrote, "I believe in intuition and inspiration. . . . At times I feel certain I am right while not knowing the reason."[4]

I know someone who was considering two job offers as an assistant, and her analytical mind told her that Job A was the far better position, but she somehow knew that she should take Job B instead. Unable to shake the inner knowledge that Job A was somehow very wrong, she took Job B. Weeks later, she learned that the person who had interviewed her for Job A had been fired. Reviewing the interview in her mind, she couldn't find any signs that supported her intuition, but knowing that it had been right, she was glad she had trusted it.

Before I begin a new creative project, I ask myself, "How will I feel if I don't complete the project?" and "What will the pain be if I fulfill my commitment and what will the pain be if I don't?" It's easy to forget that suffering can happen regardless of what you decide, including if your decision is to put off making the decision.

As you do your research using your logical, analytical abilities, don't forget your human resources: members of your Wisdom Council of Support or Creativity Support Pod. When you consult them about a decision you're trying to make, always ask, "What am I not seeing?" and be sure you're committed to listening nondefensively and taking note of what you hear. Avoid interrupting or saying, "Yes, but—" The latter means, "I don't want to take the time to consider what you're saying." Slow down and take a mindful pause. Allow there to be silence between what people say and how you respond. You might even find they have some important information because, like you, they slowed down to take a mindful pause, which triggered another insight. That might be something like "I realize I'm saying this as someone who tends to be too assertive in some situations, so take my insights for what they're worth" or "I know someone you should talk to because I'm sure they would have good ideas for you."

Your pod or council might (and should) also ask you questions like the following to help you deconstruct any false beliefs about your decision making that are causing it to feel pressured:

- What's the rush? What's the source of your sense of urgency? Are you putting unnecessary pressure on yourself when you could slow down and reduce your sense of urgency?
- What is your head telling you to do or not do?
- What is your heart/intuition/gut telling you to do or not do?

Members of your council or pod could also encourage you to share your pros, cons, pros of cons, and cons of pros—if you've used this exercise—that you can share with them.

Remember, too, that you'll want diversity among the people you consult with in your decision-making process. You might benefit from asking for feedback from someone with expertise in a particular area, someone who is good with alerting you to your emotions, someone with a different temperament—or someone who is very intuitive. Use dreamwork

EXERCISE: PROS OF CONS AND CONS OF PROS

To prod creative thinking, start by making a list of pros and cons regarding your possible decision, but instead of a list with two columns, make four columns: Pros, Cons of Pros, Cons, and Pros of Cons.

First, identify the pros and cons of making a particular choice.

Next, identify the downside of any "pro" and write it in the "cons of pros" column. For example, if your pro was "I could leave a job I've come to find stifling," your "con of pro" might be, "I would be leaving a job where I have a great team of people to work with."

Then identify the upside of any "con" and note it in the "pros of cons" column. For example, "I might have to take a pay cut" might be your con while "I could review my finances and find ways to make it on less money and even end up being in a better place financially in the long run" might be your "pro of con." A creative spin can lead you to think more deeply about the risks you would be taking with a decision. If you're spending a lot of money distracting yourself from your unhappiness with your work and life, taking a lower-paying but more rewarding job might lead you stop spending so much on distractions.

Continue with your list, and use meditations such as the Day in the Future Visualization from chapter 3, "Reclaim Your Creative Self," to get in touch with your feelings about the likely outcomes of making a change that would significantly affect your daily life.

or the gestalt technique exercise to check in with your intuition if you find those tools helpful. And consider using tarot cards to gain insights to help you in your decision making.

WORKING WITH TAROT CARDS AND YOUR INTUITION

Like dreamwork, working with tarot cards can help you get into a receptive state of open mind and tap into creative ideas and insights hidden from your conscious mind. These can be helpful as you make decisions. I sometimes work with the Osho Zen and Transformation tarot card decks, but any tarot deck you feel comfortable with will do. The symbolic meaning of the cards is the same from deck to deck, but the visual images differ, and some might appeal to you more than others.

By posing an open question such as "When it comes to my plans, what if anything am I missing?," shuffling the cards, and randomly pulling one from the deck, you perform a ritual that takes you into a more receptive mode. Turn over the card and observe which one it is. Pay attention to the mythological and archetypal symbol that appears as you enter a creative and even spiritual process of consulting your intuition. What does that card mean for you? Tarot decks come with books that explain what each card's messages can be, and you can look them up online or in other tarot interpretation books. In time, you'll come to have your own understandings of the various symbols and will be able to intuit what the card's message for you is.

For example, let's say you drew the 7 of wands, which represents dealing with some conflicts and difficulties. You might interpret it as a reminder to persevere even if your plans involve more hard work than you expected. You can check in with yourself to see how you feel about that possibility. If you're anxious, you can reflect on why you feel that way. Maybe you have a tendency to give up too easily when the going gets tough. Then you can think back to what has kept you on track in the past and set the intention to remember what strategies have worked for you so you can use them again. You might also focus on the positive, wholesome aspects of the card's message and archetypal symbolism. Maybe there are times when wrestling with a challenge is actually enjoyable, teaches you new skills, or builds your confidence. You can also think about how your Wisdom Council of Support and Creativity Support Pod might help you should you find yourself frustrated and worried that a challenge is too great for you.

By working with tarot cards in this way, like doing dreamwork, you might say you're exploring stimulation as well as changing your mind state to be more receptive—to be that of open mind where core creativity and your intuition are available to you. The idea or insight that triggers transformation might be the message to see a difficult situation from another viewpoint, or to be mindful of tendencies of yours that you often deny because they embarrass you—or something else. You can also experiment with using more than one card in "tarot spreads" or use a second or third card (drawn randomly) to gain more insights into the original message.

When I am working one-on-one or in a group setting or corporate retreat, I open up three to five different decks and ask the person which deck they would like to work with. I suggest they meditate briefly and choose the first card from the deck, laying it out before them with the back of the card showing. This first card will help them reflect on this question, "What does my unconscious/core creative self/higher self most need to explore at this very moment?" I have them place the card face up toward them. Then I suggest they choose a second card to help them reflect on the inner or outer resource they most need at this very moment to assist them with the transformation of the issue or decision they're confronting or the healing they need to do. Again, I have them place the card face up, toward them, so they can most easily view the image. Then I have them choose a third card to help them reflect on the outcome or the transformation of their issue. I find tarot cards to be a brilliant tool for providing people with a mirror that reflects back to them what is going on inside themselves—which is often hidden from the conscious mind. The meanings of the cards along with the pictures, symbols, and numbers all help the querent to reflect on their issues.

TIMING YOUR DECISION

I often see clients who are too impulsive in making decisions, either because of fear or enthusiasm. Nancy, my editor, had been unhappy as a junior editor at a major publishing house. She realized that she needed to do some research to better understand what wasn't working for her and what her options were. Was the problem the job, her boss, the department, the company, the industry—or some combination of these? She asked questions of people inside and outside of the company to learn more about their work and what they liked and disliked. Nancy came to recognize that she wanted a promotion right away to buy her some time before setting off on her ultimate goal to go freelance as a developmental editor. The latter would allow her to help authors get more in-depth guidance than in-house editors often provide and to forgo the acquisitions aspect of her job, which she didn't like.

Going freelance with little savings made her uneasy, so she hoped she would get the promotion and, with it, a raise and bonus. To that end, she made the most of an opportunity to work with two of the company's biggest authors. She provided personalized attention and gained valuable experience as she worked long hours. She also solidified her relationships with literary agents she knew and had worked with on book projects acquired by her boss, keeping in mind that if she did quit and go freelance, they might hire her to work on book proposals and manuscripts.

Like Nancy, you can decide to make a big change—leave the job, the marriage, the area of the country, the security of a full-time job with benefits, and so forth—but accept that the timing might not be right just yet. Mindful waiting, being present in the situation while the wheel turns and you take action toward the future you envision for yourself, is very different from procrastination or "phoning it in" while dreaming wistfully of a better situation. You might want to save money for the move to a new situation as you ride the wave of change, focusing on your future as well as the steps you're taking in the present to solidify it.

After many months of setting up her foundation for transformation, Nancy negotiated a promotion, raise, and bonus, but within weeks, her boss suddenly inundated her with extra work that wasn't being asked of other editors. Nancy gave her two-weeks' notice. Her boss was less than pleased at the timing—Nancy's promotion had been publicly celebrated by the staff—but the timing was right for Nancy. She now had a more impressive resume than she'd had before and relationships with literary agents who referred editorial clients to her. The bonus she had earned paid her bills as she began establishing her freelance business. She grew the business, went on to cowrite some books and do developmental editing on others, developed a solid client base, and never looked back.

IT'S ALL GOOD

Everything changes. We are always troubleshooting and tweaking, but we also have to move forth boldly even when unforeseen problems arise or the process is more troublesome than we expected. How do we know when to react to changing conditions and when to wait? By letting go of fears, tuning in to your inner wisdom, intuition, and core creativity, and only then moving forward with the decision-making process. Having developed a mindfulness practice and the ability to enter open mind to download core creativity and intuition, you now have a reliable compass to help you know what your timing should be, when you need to do more research and push back against anyone who is pressuring you, and whether you have truly given yourself enough time to make a good decision.

Will your decision matter three years from now? Seven? Twelve? Will it even matter a year from now? The weight you give your decisions can be reduced if you mindfully approach your process, knowing that "mis-takes" can lead to new opportunities.

You now have a backpack full of resources including an understanding of how the most creative and resilient people come up with ideas, shape their visions, troubleshoot, adjust as they come up against unexpected obstacles, and experience transformations that leave them feeling excited about their lives and their work. The decision before you now is how deeply to commit to adopting a regular mindfulness practice and the mind-sets and habits of highly creative people. You can set up your own plan for following through on what you've learned in this book and holding yourself accountable—or you might want to use the action plan offered in the next chapter. Whatever you decide, I hope you'll remember not to be afraid of "mis-takes" and to make a point of connecting with your intuition and the core creativity that will fuel your dreams.

Chapter Ten

The Core Creativity Action Plan

As a creativity coach, I know that having structure for starting, working on, and completing a creative project will help you avoid procrastination. However, if you're not sure what you want to create but know you want to develop greater creativity, you will also benefit from the structure of an action plan that gives you daily assignments and involves setting actionable goals to develop a vision for a creative project, present it for feedback, refine it, and set yourself up for success.

If you fall off track during the ten-week program, get right back on it the next day, recommitting to the work you promised yourself you would do. Do two days' worth of exercises in one day in order to catch up.

The plan takes ten weeks and requires you to do the following every day:

- 5–10 minutes of stretching or yogatating or doing the Body Observation Meditation from chapter 3 to observe and release any blocks to creativity that you're storing energetically and draw upon any energetically stored resources such as courage (as you read about in some of the exercises in this book).
- 20 minutes of sitting mindfulness meditation (start the first week with 5–10 minutes working up to 15–20 minutes by the second week) PLUS another 20 minutes of either mindfulness meditation or an exercise from this book. (Remember, you can try open monitoring meditation as a variation on mindfulness meditation, as I explained

back in chapter 2, "Before You Say Hello, Say Good-bye.") Each week, you'll have one or more exercises assigned. Do each at least once during that week. If you like, you can do them multiple times during the week rather than doing a second mindfulness meditation each day. You'll also have optional exercises tied in to the theme of the week, which you can use in place of that second 20 minutes of mindfulness meditation.

• Time to do some research and generating. In week 1, you'll spend at least 20 minutes engaging in a creative art without judgment. After that, at the very least, schedule an hour for that engagement over the course of each of the next nine weeks. However, if you can set aside more time for it, do so!

You can also add an optional 10 to 20 minutes of working with the Body Observation Meditation, a vision board (see chapter 7, "Mind-sets and Habits of Highly Creative People," for instructions), tarot cards (see chapter 9, "Mindful Decision Making," or a dream that you suspect has yielded insights for you (see chapter 5, "Absorbing Creative Stimulation and Getting into Open Mind Consciousness").

The mindfulness practice is extremely important for this plan to work for you. Note that as you practice mindfulness meditation throughout the ten weeks of the core creativity action plan, you'll be aiming for a blend of mindful awareness of your breathing and mindful awareness of creative ideas flowing into you. You might not have to interrupt yourself to record those ideas—you might be able to remember them all at the end of your session. After your meditation, be sure to record them if you didn't stop to do so.

I have not incorporated the exercises from chapter 9, "Mindful Decision Making," into the action plan, but if you find that developing greater creativity or a creative project causes you to have to make a difficult decision, schedule into your planner time to do the exercises from that chapter.

I strongly encourage you to schedule your assigned exercises immediately after reading about the action plan and to check it every morning as soon as you wake up and every night before you go to bed to remind yourself of your commitment.

Some people can hold themselves accountable for a ten-week program and their commitments to themselves, but most people need some sort of check-in. You can ask someone from your Wisdom Council of Support to agree to check in with you at the end of each week to make sure you did your assignments, or your accountability partner can be a therapist or coach. Later in the program, you might decide to assemble a Creativity Support Pod and have a member of it to be your accountability partner.

You might want to start working the action plan on a Sunday and maybe even at the beginning of a month, after a vacation or a birthday or even January 1 as a New Year's resolution. In this way, you set yourself up to make the start of the action plan a special occasion you look forward to and are committing to 100 percent.

If you would like a PDF that provides a simple summary of the plan, go to https://ronaldalexander.com/core-creativity-action-plan/.

WEEK 1: COMMIT TO NEW HABITS AND THE PLAN

This week, you'll commit to increasing your tolerance for sitting mindfulness meditation. Remember, for the first few days, you can begin with just 5 or 10 minutes for your first session, doing a few minutes of stretching or yogatating beforehand to help your mind calm its choppy waters and reduce internal distractions. Your second mindfulness session can be a 15- to 20-minute walking meditation, but by the end of the week, make sure you have done your assigned meditation, which should take about the same amount of time, at least once. The idea is to consistently do a 15- to 20-minute session of mindfulness meditation or another meditation/visualization/exercise from this book every day for ten weeks.

If you already meditate for 15 or 20 minutes twice a day consistently, excellent! You might want to continue that and add on top of it each of the assigned exercises at least once this week.

Assigned Exercise #1: Gestalt Inquiry Technique Exercise from Chapter 5

To learn if you have any resistance to your commitment, use the gestalt technique to ask your head, heart, and wisdom what they can tell you. What thoughts about a creative project or vision are getting in your way? How do you feel about this endeavor? What does your wise self have to say about it? Write about what you learned as a result of using the gestalt technique to gain insights into any resistance you're experiencing. While you might not think you're resistant to doing the ten-week program, you might well find after a few days of disciplined adherence to your plan that you start skipping meditation sessions, giving yourself any number of excuses. By using the gestalt technique to uncover any resistance, you're more likely to follow through with your commitment.

Assigned Exercise #2: Body Observation Meditation from Chapter 3

Begin the Body Observation Meditation with the intention of finding any blocks to creativity and tapping into any energy that motivates you to be creative. If you miss doing your daily exercises one day, as I said earlier, double up the next day. But also make sure you use the gestalt technique and Body Observation Meditation with the intention of discovering any unconscious resistance that caused you to skip your exercises.

When you find an energetic block to being creative, remember, it might feel like a heavy spot or a constriction, but you might experience it differently. You might see in your mind's eye a symbol, such as a knot by your stomach, or hear words or sounds that tell you that in this area of your body and energy field, you are holding onto resistance. Simply observe that resistance to see what happens. Does it change in quality or intensity? Does an insight arise? Write about your experience afterward.

Assigned Exercise #3: Freewrite, Draw, Paint, Dance, Sing, or Play a Musical Instrument for at Least 20 Minutes

If you find you're negatively judging yourself, remember that mistakes are merely "mis-takes," and no one is watching you or giving you feedback. And even if you think you have no skills and no talent, engage in the creative art anyway. The point is simply to click on the zip file, so to speak: to generate ideas so that you might enter a state of open mind. If you don't, no worries. The other exercises in this program will help you release any constrictions and prime you to experience open mind.

Accountability Assignment: Procure an accountability partner who can work with you starting at the end of week 2 to make sure you did your assignments in the program.

Also, use the Body Observation Meditation, the Gestalt Inquiry Technique, a vision board, and tarot cards if you feel these tools will help you.

WEEK 2: DISSOLVE ANY HIDDEN RESISTANCE

Just as in week 1, you will stretch or do yogatating for few minutes before doing each of your two 15- to 20-minute meditation sessions, making one of them a session of sitting mindfulness meditation and the other the same or one of the assigned exercises for this week. Pay attention to any distractions that make it difficult to stick to your commitment, and use your creativity to find ways to rid yourself of them. You can again use the Gestalt Inquiry Technique and the Body Observation Meditation to get to the bottom of any hidden resistance that is sabotaging you.

Assigned Exercise #1: Return to the Scene to Change It Visualization from Chapter 3

Identify an event related to being creative that has caused you resistance now or in the past. For example, you might remember a parent telling you not to "waste time" drawing in a sketchbook or taking a high school class you were very interested in but that wouldn't help you get into a "good college." You might remember a time when you hit a plateau with your art and someone inadvertently validated your fear that you had peaked and shouldn't expect to experience success again. Go back to the scene and imagine it playing out differently.

Optional Exercise: Perfect Completion Visualization from Chapter 2

If you find yourself pining for an old creative project or a time in your life when core creativity was flowing and you were "in the zone," do this visualization as one of your weekly exercises.

Creativity Assignment: Spend at least an hour doing research, absorbing, and generating ideas related to your creative project or ideas for one.

Accountability Assignment: Check in with your accountability partner at the end of the week.

Also, use the Body Observation Meditation, the Gestalt Inquiry Technique, a vision board, and tarot cards if you feel these tools will help you.

WEEK 3: FIND SUPPORT FROM WITHIN AND OUTSIDE YOURSELF FOR YOUR CREATIVITY TO UNFOLD

Week 3's focus is on receiving support and trusting your unconscious resources. For the rest of the ten weeks, continue doing 5 to 10 minutes of stretching or yogatating, 15 to 20 minutes of mindfulness meditation or another exercise twice a day, and at least 20 minutes of engaging in a creative art.

Assigned Exercise #1: Consulting a Mentor
Visualization from Chapter 4

Remember that the imaginary mentor you're dialoguing with in this visualization represents your wise inner self that may give you insights that you wouldn't have had if you'd simply thought about "What would a highly talented and successful screenwriter or musician tell me about my own creative expressions?"

Optional Exercise: Releasing Jealousy
Visualization from Chapter 4

Use this exercise if you feel envious of someone you see as more creative and successful than you are. Keep in mind that creativity is not a competition, and consider rereading chapter 7 to see how a mind-set or habit of mind might be contributing to your jealousy and to refresh yourself on the mind-sets of highly creative people.

Optional Exercise: Assemble a Creativity Support Pod and Schedule the First Meeting

If you're interested in doing a creative project, even if you don't know what it is yet, consider assembling a Creativity Support Pod that would meet regularly as described in chapter 4, "Support and Collaboration." Do the preliminary work by finding at least two people willing to serve in this pod. You might ask them to suggest members and to contact them to see if they're interested. Start to set up the schedule and meeting time, aiming to have at least six members of the pod. Communicate the rules to all members.

Creativity Assignment: Spend at least an hour doing research, absorbing, and generating ideas related to your creative project or ideas for one.

Accountability Assignment: Check in with your accountability partner at the end of the week.

Also, use the Body Observation Meditation, the Gestalt Inquiry Technique, a vision board, and tarot cards if you feel these tools will help you.

WEEK 4: CREATE AND ARTICULATE YOUR VISION

Your vision might be a creative project you can complete by the end of the ten-week program or a vision for beginning the work of starting a business or organization or reinventing your everyday life. This week, you will decide what the project is, setting an attainable goal to be completed by the end of your ten weeks. For example, you might decide to set up a home workspace and an Etsy store, or research moving across the country to pursue a dream career or activity so that you can have a solid plan by the end of the ten weeks of the Core Creativity Action Plan. You might decide you'll come up with a screenplay treatment and two scenes, or an idea for a painting and a sketch for it. Whatever you decide on as your project, it's important that your vision be concrete and achievable.

Assigned Exercise #1: Day in the Future Visualization from Chapter 3

As I explained in the instructions for this exercise, if you feel somewhat uncomfortable with what you're experiencing in your mind's eye while you're doing it, that's okay. Explore through journaling why that might be—and consider doing the exercise again a little further into the future to see if it's easier to enjoy it. So, for example, if you're imagining having your first showing of your artwork, you might also want to create in your mind a day in the future when you're having yet another art show, having done one several times before.

Assigned Exercise #2: No-Self Way into Core Creativity Meditation from Chapter 6

Immerse yourself in a state of no-self, letting your ego move completely out of the way so that you can experience a core creativity download.

Assigned Exercise #3: Write Out Your Vision

Commit your goal to paper, as if it were a mission statement. Write at least a paragraph so that your vision is articulated with details. Your vision should be specific and concrete. If you realize you've come up with a vision that you can't manifest by the end of the ten-week program, then specify exactly what you're going to accomplish toward your larger goal. You're not going to quit your day job and become a sculptor by the end of the Core Creativity Action Plan program, but you can choose to start with a simple project to complete. For example, you might aim to set up a workspace, buy supplies, envision your first sculpture, and begin working on it.

Creativity Assignment: Spend at least an hour doing research, absorbing, and generating ideas related to your creative project or ideas for one.

Accountability Assignment: Check in with your accountability partner at the end of the week.

Also, use the Body Observation Meditation, the Gestalt Inquiry Technique, a vision board, and tarot cards if you feel these tools will help you.

WEEK 5: CREATE ACTIONABLE GOALS AND BEGIN RESEARCHING, ABSORBING, AND GENERATING TO MEET THEM

To bring your vision into manifestation, you'll articulate specific goals for weeks 5 through 10 at the beginning of this week.

Goal-Setting Assignment: On day 1 of week 5, write out your goals for this week as well as for weeks 6 through 10.

Creativity Assignment: Spend at least an hour doing research, absorbing, and generating ideas related to your creative project or ideas for one.

Accountability Assignment: Check in with your accountability partner at the end of the week.

Also, use the Body Observation Meditation, the Gestalt Inquiry Technique, a vision board, and tarot cards if you feel these tools will help you.

WEEK 6: ARTICULATE YOUR WINNING FORMULA AND GIVE YOURSELF CREDIT FOR MAKING PROGRESS

At the beginning of week 6, write out any winning formulas you've used in the past and any that others have used successfully and reflect on them. Does one seem to be the right winning formula to use to finish your creative project in a timely and satisfactory way? Do you have to customize or change it in some way? For example, has your situation changed since the last time you used a particular winning formula? Or, is there a reason you can't borrow someone else's winning formula to achieve success? What could you alter in that formula to make it work for you given your circumstances right now? Answer these questions in a journal or notebook and revisit your vision. Do you need to further define and clarify it for yourself now that you've got a winning formula to use as a template? Can the winning formula help you refine your goals to be more specific and achievable?

Winning Formula Assignment: Write out winning formulas you know of and reflect on them. Then identify the winning formula you're going to use to guide you in manifesting your vision or creative project.

Assigned Exercise #1: Mindful Patience Meditation from Chapter 7

Even if you don't feel impatient, do this exercise at least once during week 6.

Assigned Exercise #2: Mindful Self-Compassion Visualization from Chapter 6

As you're working on your vision, it's important to be enthusiastic, but you also must have patience and self-compassion. By working with the meditations that allow you to let go of any sense of anxiety about the pace of your project and any negative self-judgments, you'll make it easier to keep core creativity flowing.

Assigned Exercise #3: Write about Your Progress and Give Yourself Credit for Specific Achievements

Take time to sit with the progress you've made so far, and cultivate a sense of satisfaction and pride. You might reward yourself for making progress so far by buying yourself something or giving yourself a break from chores that tend to be unpleasant or draining. However, regardless of any reward you give yourself, make sure to write about your progress and what helped or hindered you as well as what you did to overcome any obstacles. Sit with the feeling of accomplishment.

Creativity Assignment: Spend at least an hour doing research, absorbing, and generating ideas related to your creative project or ideas for one.

Accountability Assignment: Check in with your accountability partner at the end of the week.

Also, use the Body Observation Meditation, the Gestalt Inquiry Technique, a vision board, and tarot cards if you feel these tools will help you.

WEEK 7: PRESENT YOUR CREATIVE PROJECT OR PLAN

Ready yourself to present, at the end of the week, your first draft of your creative project or plan to your Creativity Support Pod or someone in your Wisdom Council of Support who is encouraging. The latter might be someone in your life who has successfully completed a creative project. If your accountability partner isn't part of your Creativity Support Pod and isn't necessarily someone you would like to get feedback from, you don't have to present your project to this person, but you do have to tell them what you've completed. For example, if you wrote a summary of your memoir and a few sample stories, you would let them know, but you might not ask them to read what you've written.

When you present your project, ask for supportive attention from those you're presenting to and feedback afterward. Explain that the feedback you want is one to three positive observations about it and one positive suggestion for what to work on that would assist you or the project to make it better. If you feel confident enough to handle more than one constructive piece of feedback, ask for two or even three.

After receiving feedback, make the time to do a visualization of what needs to be done next to improve the project. Sit quietly and breathe in and out seven to twelve long, deep, slow breaths as you relax and pay attention in your mind's eye to the third eye space between both eyebrows. Quietly await a natural unfolding from your creative unconscious of what to make of the feedback you've received and how to use that feedback to improve your creative work or further define and refine your vision. What new possibilities bubble up now that you've received feedback? Pay close attention to what arises. Do you get the message that you need to do more research? Let go of something? Reflect on what might be missing and could be added? Go in a different direction? Enhance something that's working but that you need more of? Practice more? As always, whether it's an inner knowing, words or sounds or sensations or auditory information that comes to you, observe it and afterward journal about it to better understand how you might apply the insight.

Assigned Exercise: Mindful Self-Compassion Visualization from Chapter 6.

Presentation Assignment: Present your creative project or vision and receive feedback.

Creativity Assignment: Spend at least an hour doing research, absorbing, and generating ideas related to your creative project or ideas for one.

Accountability Assignment: Check in with your accountability partner at the end of the week by presenting your project or plan.

Also, use the Body Observation Meditation, the Gestalt Inquiry Technique, a vision board, and tarot cards if you feel these tools will help you.

WEEKS 8 AND 9: REFINEMENT OF
YOUR PROJECT OR PLAN

During weeks 8 and 9, you won't be gathering any more input or feedback. You're honing your project with the plan of completing it in week 10. Be sure to check in with your accountability partner at the end of each week.

Refinement Assignment: Hone Your Project or Plan

Make a list of the strengths and weaknesses of your plan to guide you in your refinement work. Schedule at least ten hours a week for the refinement work—and this is on top of your twice daily meditation.

Accountability Assignment: Check in with your accountability partner at the end of each week.

Also, use the Body Observation Meditation, the Gestalt Inquiry Technique, a vision board, and tarot cards if you feel these tools will help you.

WEEK 10: COMPLETION OF YOUR PROJECT
OR PLAN FOR THE PROJECT

During week 10, unlike in other weeks when you checked in with your accountability partner at the end of the week, check in midweek to be sure you're on track for completion and presentation—to members of your Wisdom Council of Support or Creativity Support Pod—at the end of the week. I suggest that at the beginning of week 10, you write out a checklist of what you absolutely must get done by your midweek check-in and by the last day of the week.

Bring your creative project or plan back to the Creativity Support Pod to show them what you did with the ideas and feedback they offered you. Their role now is simply to affirm, acknowledge, and encourage you.

Final Presentation Project: Present your creative project or plan, as described.

Also, use the Body Observation Meditation, the Gestalt Inquiry Technique, a vision board, and tarot cards if you feel these tools will help you.

Appendix

The Core Creativity Action Plan

Ronald Alexander, PhD

Adapted from the book Core Creativity: The Mindful Way to Unlock Your Creative Self *by Ronald Alexander, PhD*

WEEK 1: COMMIT TO NEW HABITS AND THE PLAN

Daily:

- 5–10 minutes of stretching or yogatating or doing the Body Observation Meditation from chapter 3 from *Core Creativity: The Mindful Way to Unlock Your Creative Self.*
- Sitting mindfulness meditation for 5–10 minutes, working up to 15–20 minutes by the end of the week, PLUS another 20 minutes of either mindfulness meditation or an exercise from *Core Creativity.*
- At least 20 minutes engaging in a creative art without judgment.

Over the course of the week:

- *Accountability Assignment*: Procure an accountability partner who can work with you starting at the end of week 2 to make sure you did all your assignments in the program.
- *Assigned Exercise #1*: Gestalt Inquiry Technique exercise from chapter 5

- *Assigned Exercise #2*: Body Observation Meditation from chapter 3
- *Assigned Exercise #3*: Freewrite, draw, paint, dance, sing, or play a musical instrument for at least 20 minutes

OPTIONAL: Also, use the Gestalt Inquiry Technique, the Body Observation Meditation, a vision board, and tarot cards if you feel these tools will help you.

WEEK 2: DISSOLVE ANY HIDDEN RESISTANCE

Daily:

- 5–10 minutes of stretching or yogatating or doing the Body Observation Meditation
- 15–20 minutes sitting mindfulness meditation, PLUS another 20 minutes of either mindfulness meditation or an exercise from *Core Creativity.*
- At least 20 minutes engaging in a creative art without judgment.

Over the course of the week:

- *Assigned Exercise #1:* Return to the Scene to Change It Visualization from chapter 3
- OPTIONAL: Perfect Completion Visualization from chapter 2
- OPTIONAL: 10 to 20 minutes of working with the Body Observation Meditation, a vision board (see chapter 7, "Mind-sets and Habits of Highly Creative People," for instructions), tarot cards, or a dream that you suspect has yielded insights for you.
- *Accountability Assignment:* Check in with your accountability partner at the end of the week.
- *Creativity Assignment:* Spend at least an hour doing research, absorbing, and generating ideas related to your creative project or ideas for one.

WEEK 3: FIND SUPPORT FROM WITHIN AND OUTSIDE YOURSELF FOR YOUR CREATIVITY TO UNFOLD

Daily:

- 5–10 minutes of stretching or yogatating or doing the Body Observation Meditation
- 15–20 minutes sitting mindfulness meditation, PLUS another 20 minutes of either mindfulness meditation or an exercise from *Core Creativity.*
- At least 20 minutes engaging in a creative art without judgment.

Over the course of the week:

- *Assigned Exercise #1:* Consulting a Mentor Visualization from chapter 4
- OPTIONAL: Releasing Jealousy Visualization from chapter 4
- OPTIONAL: Assemble a Creativity Support Pod and schedule the first meeting.
- *Creativity Assignment*: Spend at least an hour doing research, absorbing, and generating ideas related to your creative project or ideas for one.
- *Accountability Assignment*: Check in with your accountability partner at the end of the week.

Also, use the Gestalt Inquiry Technique, the Body Observation Meditation, a vision board, and tarot cards if you feel these tools will help you.

WEEK 4: CREATE AND ARTICULATE YOUR VISION

Daily:

- 5–10 minutes of stretching or yogatating or doing the Body Observation Meditation
- 15–20 minutes sitting mindfulness meditation, PLUS another 20 minutes of either mindfulness meditation or an exercise from *Core Creativity.*
- At least 20 minutes engaging in a creative art without judgment.

Over the course of the week:

* *Assigned Exercise #1*: Day in the Future Visualization from chapter 3
* *Assigned Exercise #2*: No-Self Way into Core Creativity Meditation from chapter 6
* *Assigned Exercise #3*: Write out your vision.
* *Creativity Assignment*: Spend at least an hour doing research, absorbing, and generating ideas related to your creative project or ideas for one.
* *Accountability Assignment*: Check in with your accountability partner at the end of the week.

Also, use the Body Observation Meditation, the Gestalt Inquiry Technique, a vision board, and tarot cards if you feel these tools will help you.

WEEK 5: CREATE ACTIONABLE GOALS AND BEGIN RESEARCHING, ABSORBING, AND GENERATING TO MEET THEM

Daily:

* 5–10 minutes of stretching or yogatating or doing the Body Observation Meditation
* 15–20 minutes sitting mindfulness meditation, PLUS another 20 minutes of either mindfulness meditation or an exercise from *Core Creativity*.
* At least 20 minutes engaging in a creative art without judgment.

Over the course of the week:

* *Goal-Setting Assignment*: On day 1 of week 5, write out your goals for this week as well as for weeks 6 through 10.
* *Creativity Assignment*: Spend at least an hour doing research, absorbing, and generating ideas related to your creative project or ideas for one.

- *Accountability Assignment*: Check in with your accountability partner at the end of the week.

Also, use the Body Observation Meditation, the Gestalt Inquiry Technique, a vision board, and tarot cards if you feel these tools will help you.

WEEK 6: ARTICULATE YOUR WINNING FORMULA AND GIVE YOURSELF CREDIT FOR MAKING PROGRESS

Daily:

- 5–10 minutes of stretching or yogatating or doing the Body Observation Meditation
- 15–20 minutes sitting mindfulness meditation, PLUS another 20 minutes of either mindfulness meditation or an exercise from *Core Creativity*.
- At least 20 minutes engaging in a creative art without judgment.

Over the course of the week:

- *Winning Formula Assignment*: Write out winning formulas you know of and reflect on them. Then identify the winning formula you're going to use to guide you in manifesting your vision or creative project.
- *Assigned Exercise #1*: Mindful Patience Meditation from chapter 7
- *Assigned Exercise #2*: Mindful Self-Compassion Visualization from chapter 6
- *Assigned Exercise #3*: Write about your progress and give yourself credit for specific achievements.
- *Creativity Assignment*: Spend at least an hour doing research, absorbing, and generating ideas related to your creative project or ideas for one.
- *Accountability Assignment*: Check in with your accountability partner at the end of the week.

Also, use the Body Observation Meditation, the Gestalt Inquiry Technique, a vision board, and tarot cards if you feel these tools will help you.

WEEK 7: PRESENT YOUR CREATIVE PROJECT OR PLAN

Daily:

- 5–10 minutes of stretching or yogatating or doing the Body Observation Meditation
- 15–20 minutes sitting mindfulness meditation, PLUS another 20 minutes of either mindfulness meditation or an exercise from *Core Creativity*.
- At least 20 minutes engaging in a creative art without judgment.

Over the course of the week:

- *Assigned exercise*: Mindful Self-Compassion Visualization from chapter 6.
- *Presentation Assignment*: Present your creative project or vision and receive feedback.
- *Creativity Assignment*: Spend at least an hour doing research, absorbing, and generating ideas related to your creative project or ideas for one.
- *Accountability Assignment*: Check in with your accountability partner at the end of the week by presenting your project or plan.

Also, use the Body Observation Meditation, the Gestalt Inquiry Technique, a vision board, and tarot cards if you feel these tools will help you.

WEEKS 8 AND 9: REFINEMENT OF YOUR PROJECT OR PLAN

- 5–10 minutes of stretching or yogatating or doing the Body Observation Meditation
- 15–20 minutes sitting mindfulness meditation, PLUS another 20 minutes of either mindfulness meditation or an exercise from *Core Creativity*.
- At least 20 minutes engaging in a creative art without judgment.

Over the course of the weeks:

* *Refinement Assignment*: Hone your project or plan. Make a list of the strengths and weaknesses of your plan to guide you in your refinement work. Do refinement work at least ten hours a week—and this is on top of your twice daily meditation.
* *Accountability Assignment*: Check in with your accountability partner at the end of each week.

Also, use the Body Observation Meditation, the Gestalt Inquiry Technique, a vision board, and tarot cards if you feel these tools will help you.

WEEK 10: COMPLETION OF YOUR PROJECT OR PLAN FOR THE PROJECT

Daily:

* 5–10 minutes of stretching or yogatating or doing the Body Observation Meditation
* 15–20 minutes sitting mindfulness meditation, PLUS another 20 minutes of either mindfulness meditation or an exercise from *Core Creativity*.
* At least 20 minutes engaging in a creative art without judgment.

Over the course of the week:

* *Accountability Assignment:* Day 1, write a checklist of what you absolutely must get done by midweek and by the last day of the week. Check in with your accountability partner midweek.
* *Final Presentation Project*: Present your creative project or plan, as described.

Also, use the Body Observation Meditation, the Gestalt Inquiry Technique, a vision board, and tarot cards if you feel these tools will help you.

Notes

CHAPTER ONE

1. Amanda Van Nuys, "New LinkedIn Research: Upskill Your Employees with the Skills Companies Need Most in 2020," LinkedIn Learning Blog, December 28, 2019. https://www.linkedin.com/business/learning/blog/learning-and-development/most-in-demand-skills-2020.

2. AMA Staff, "AMA Critical Skills Survey: Workers Need Higher Level Skills to Succeed in the 21st Century," American Management Association, January 24, 2019. https://www.amanet.org/articles/ama-critical-skills-survey-workers-need-higher-level-skills-to-succeed-in-the-21st-century/.

3. David Slocum, "The Rise of Creativity as a Key Quality in Modern Leadership," *Forbes,* January 27, 2015. https://www.forbes.com/sites/berlinschoolofcreativeleadership/2015/01/27/the-rise-of-creativity-is-a-key-quality-in-modern-leadership/?sh=5295b337d1ad.

4. Terence McKenna, "The Purpose of Psychedelics," YouTube, June 7, 2014. Accessed August 30, 2021. https://www.youtube.com/watch?v=rXQfE3W4wVY.

5. R. Keith Sawyer, "Creativity and Mental Illness: Is There a Link?" *The Huffington Post,* January 2, 2012, updated January 23, 2014. https://www.huffpost.com/entry/creativity-and-mental-ill_b_2059806.

6. Roger Beaty, "Route of Creativity Revealed by fMRI," *The Conversation,* January 17, 2018. https://www.technologynetworks.com/neuroscience/news/brain-imaging-reveals-why-some-people-are-more-creative-than-others-296433. Also, Roger E. Beaty et al., "Robust Prediction of Individual Creative Ability from Brain Functional Connectivity," *Proceedings of the*

National Academy of Sciences, January 30, 2018. https://doi.org/10.1073
.pnas.1713532115. https://www.pnas.org/content/115/5/1087.

7. Rohini Venkatraman, "Science Says We Get Less Creative as We Age.
Prove It Wrong by Doing 1 of These 3 Things," *Inc.,* August 29, 2017. https://
www.inc.com/rohini-venkatraman/science-says-we-get-less-creative-as-we
-age-prove-.html.

8. Britta K. Hölzel et al., 2010. "Stress Reduction Correlates with Structural Changes in the Amygdala," *Social Cognitive and Affective Neuroscience*
5, no. 1 (March 2010): 11–17. https://doi.org/10.1093/scan/nsp034. Published
September 23, 2009. https://academic.oup.com/scan/article/5/1/11/1728269.

9. Brigid Schulte, "Harvard Neuroscientist: Meditation Not Only Reduces
Stress, Here's How It Changes Your Brain," *The Washington Post,* May
26, 2015. https://www.washingtonpost.com/news/inspired-life/wp/2015/05/26
/harvard-neuroscientist-meditation-not-only-reduces-stress-it-literally-changes
-your-brain/. Referring to Britta K. Hölzel et al., "Mindfulness Practice Leads
to Increases in Regional Brain Gray Matter Density," *Psychiatry Research* 191,
no. 1 (January 30, 2011): 36–43. https://www.ncbi.nlm.nih.gov/pmc/articles
/PMC3004979/.

10. In his groundbreaking book *Flow,* Mihaly Csikszentmihalyi wrote, "In
our studies, we found that every flow activity, whether it involved competition, chance, or any other dimension of experience, had this in common: *It
provided a sense of discovery, a creative feeling of transporting the person into
a new reality. It pushed the person to higher levels of performance, and led to
undreamed-of states of consciousness*" (italics mine). Mihaly Csikszentmihalyi, *Flow: The Psychology of Optimal Experience* (New York: HarperCollins
Publishers, 1990), 74.

11. Maura Boldrini et al., "Human Hippocampal Neurogenesis Persists
throughout Aging," *Cell Stem Cell* 22, no. 4 (April 5, 2018): 589–99. doi:
10.1016/j.stem.2018.03.015. https://pubmed.ncbi.nlm.nih.gov/29625071/.

12. Dean Keith Simonton, "Does Creativity Decline with Age?" *Scientific
American,* March 1, 2016. https://www.scientificamerican.com/article/does
-creativity-decline-with-age/.

13. Jill Suttie, "Five Ways Mindfulness Meditation Is Good for Your Health,"
Greater Good Magazine, Mind and Body section, October 24, 2018. https://
greatergood.berkeley.edu/article/item/five_ways_mindfulness_meditation
_is_good_for_your_health.

14. Heather L. Stuckey and Jeremy Nobel, "The Connection between
Art, Healing, and Public Health: A Review of Current Literature," *American
Journal of Public Health,* February 2010. https://ajph.aphapublications.org
/doi/10.2105/AJPH.2008.156497.

15. Anne Bolwerk, "How Art Changes Your Brain: Differential Effects of
Visual Art Production and Cognitive Art Evaluation on Functional Brain Con-

nectivity," *PLoS ONE* 9, no. 7 (July 1, 2014): e101035. https://journals.plos.org/plosone/article?id=10.1371/journal.pone.0101035.

16. Cathy Malchiodi, PhD, "Creativity as a Wellness Practice," *Psychology Today*, December 31, 2015. https://www.psychologytoday.com/us/blog/arts-and-health/201512/creativity-wellness-practice; and Rosebud O. Roberts et al., "Risk and Protective Factors for Cognitive Impairment in Persons Aged 85 Years and Older," *Neurology* 84, no. 18 (May 5, 2015): 1854–61. https://www.ncbi.nlm.nih.gov/pmc/articles/PMC4433468/.

17. Sir Ken Robinson, "Do Schools Kill Creativity?" *TED 2006*, February 2006. https://www.ted.com/talks/sir_ken_robinson_do_schools_kill_creativity?language=en.

18. Albert Einstein, *Cosmic Religion: With Other Opinions and Aphorisms* (New York: Covici-Friede, 1931, republished New York: Dover Publications, 2009), 97.

19. Cody Fern, interview with the author, October 14, 2020.

20. Elizabeth Gilbert, *Big Magic: Creative Living beyond Fear* (New York: Penguin Random House, 2015), 42–57.

21. David Seltzer, interview with the author, July 25, 2021.

CHAPTER TWO

1. Herbert Benson, with Miriam Z. Klipper, *The Relaxation Response* (New York: William Morrow and Company, Inc., 1975).

2. Lorenzo S. Colzato et al., "Meditate to Create: The Impact of Focused Attention and Open Monitoring Training on Convergent and Divergent Thinking," *Frontiers in Psychology* 3, no. 116 (April 18, 2012). doi: 10.3389/fpsyg.2012.00116. https://www.frontiersin.org/articles/10.3389/fpsyg.2012.00116/full.

3. Cody Fern, interview with the author, January 15, 2021.

4. Mary Hunger et al., "Urban Nature Experiences Reduce Stress in the Context of Daily Life Based on Salivary Biomarkers," *Frontiers in Psychology* 10, no. 722 (April 4, 2019). https://doi.org/10.3389/fpsyg.2019.00722. https://www.frontiersin.org/articles/10.3389/fpsyg.2019.00722/full.

5. "The more mindful we are, the less self-conscious we are." Ellen J. Langer, *On Becoming an Artist: Reinventing Yourself through Mindful Creativity* (New York: Ballantine Books, 2005), 40.

6. Ideas.Ted.Com, "What Making Music Does to Your Brain," November 10, 2015. Retrieved August 4, 2021. https://ideas.ted.com/what-making-music-does-to-your-brain/.

7. Walter Everett, *The Beatles as Musicians: Revolver through the Anthology* (Oxford: Oxford University Press, 1999), 464–65.

8. *Playboy*'s Beatles Interviews Database. *Playboy* 1980, p. 1. http://www.beatlesinterviews.org/db1980.jlpb.beatles.html.

9. Jessica Nguyen and Eric Brymer, "Nature-Based Guided Imagery as an Intervention for State Anxiety," *Frontiers in Psychology* 9, no. 1858 (October 2, 2018). doi:10.3389/fpsyg.2018.01858. https://www.ncbi.nlm.nih.gov/pmc/articles/PMC6176042/.

CHAPTER THREE

1. Peter A. Levine, *Waking the Tiger: Healing Trauma* (Berkeley, CA: North Atlantic Books, 1997).

2. Bessel A. van der Kolk, *The Body Keeps the Score: Brain, Mind and Body in the Healing of Trauma* (New York: Penguin Books, 2014), 98.

3. Ibid., 53.

4. Ibid., 285.

5. Bessel A. van der Kolk et al., "Yoga as an Adjunctive Treatment for Posttraumatic Stress Disorder: A Randomized, Controlled Trial," *Journal of Clinical Psychiatry* 75, no. 6 (June 2014): 559–65. doi:10.4088/JCP.13m08561. https://pubmed.ncbi.nlm.nih.gov/25004196/.

6. David Seltzer, interview with the author.

CHAPTER FOUR

1. Ronnie Landfield, interview with the author, October 14, 2020.

2. Jonathan Scales, interview with the author, November 20, 2020.

3. Aron Krerowicz, Flip Side Beatles blog, "The History of Strawberry Fields Forever, Part 12: The Splice," drawn from Geoff Emerick with Howard Massey, *Here, There and Everywhere: My Life Recording the Music of The Beatles* (New York, NY: Gotham Books, 2006); and from George Martin with William Pearson, *With a Little Help from My Friends: The Making of Sgt. Pepper* (Boston, MA: Little Brown and Company, 1994). https://www.aaronkrerowicz.com/beatles-blog/the-history-of-strawberry-fields-forever-part-12-the-splice.

4. Amy Ziering, interview with the author, July 3, 2021.

5. Ibid.

6. Julian Lennon, interview with the author. https://www.huffpost.com/entry/mindful-music-the-creatio_b_3548016.

7. Jodi Long, interview with the author, December 24, 2020.

8. Jean Stein, interviewer, "William Faulkner, The Art of Fiction #12," *The Paris Review* 12 (Spring 1956). https://www.theparisreview.org/interviews/4954/the-art-of-fiction-no-12-william-faulkner.

9. Jodi Long, interview with the author, December 24, 2020.

CHAPTER FIVE

1. William James, *The Varieties of Religious Experience*. Originally published by Longmans, Green and Co. 1902 (New York: Random House, The Modern Library, 1929), 378.

2. CinemaMusic55 channel, "Paul Simon on Songwriting," YouTube, posted October 9, 2021. https://youtu.be/czSfvauFtQc.

3. Fredrik Scavlan, "Paul Simon: Evidently My Expression Says There's Something Wrong," SVT/NRK/Skavlan, Skavlan TV, YouTube, posted September 30, 2016. https://youtu.be/aG1PK_rLw8M.

4. Jodi Long, interview with the author.

5. Yaro Starak, interview with the author.

6. Judith Orloff, *Guide to Intuitive Healing: 5 Steps to Physical, Emotional and Sexual Wellness* (New York: Harmony Books, 2001), xiv.

7. Cody Fern, interview with the author.

8. Joe Keohane, "The Hemi Q&A: James Taylor," *Hemispheres* magazine, June 2015, 72.

9. Amit Ray, *Meditation: Insights and Inspiration* (inner-light-in.com, Inner Light Publishers: 2015), 57.

10. Cody Fern, interview with the author.

11. Rhonda Bryant, written statement provided to the author.

12. Genevive R. Meredith et al., "Minimum Time Dose in Nature to Positively Impact the Mental Health of College-Aged Students, and How to Measure It: A Scoping Review," *Frontiers in Psychology* 10, no. 2942 (January 14, 2020). doi:10.3389/fpsyg.2019.02942. https://www.frontiersin.org/articles/10.3389/fpsyg.2019.02942/full.

13. Gregory N. Bratman et al., "Nature Experience Reduces Rumination and Subgenual Prefrontal Cortex Activation," *Proceedings of the National Academy of Sciences of the United States of America* 112, no. 28 (July 14, 2015): 8567–72. https://doi.org/10.1073/pnas.1510459112. https://www.pnas.org/content/112/28/8567.abstract.

14. Mason Currey, *Daily Rituals: How Artists Work* (New York: Alfred A. Knopf, 2013).

15. Cody Fern, interview with the author.

16. Jeff Opperman, "Taylor Swift Is Singing Us Back to Nature," *New York Times,* March 12, 2021. https://www.nytimes.com/2021/03/12/opinion/taylor -swift-grammys-nature-lyrics.html?searchResultPosition=1.

17. Ruth Ann Atchley et al., "Creativity in the Wild: Improving Creative Reasoning through Immersion in Natural Settings," *PLoS ONE* 7, no. 12 (December 12, 2012): e51474. https://journals.plos.org/plosone/article?id=10.1371 /journal.pone.0051474.

18. James Taylor on his process of songwriting. Joe Keohane, "The Hemi Q&A: James Taylor," *Hemispheres* magazine, June 2015, p. 71. https:// s3.amazonaws.com/inklive-emags/emagStorage/hemi/2015/jun2/files/assets /basic-html/index.html#83.

19. Robbie Robertson on the creative process. Daniel Roher, director, *Once Were Brothers,* Magnolia Pictures, 2019.

20. Brian Hiatt, "True Bruce: Springsteen Goes Deep, from Early Trauma to the Future of E Street: Rocker Opens Up about His Life, Expanding on Revelations in Candid New Memoir 'Born to Run,'" *Rolling Stone,* October 5, 2016. https://www.rollingstone.com/music/music-features/true-bruce -springsteen-goes-deep-from-early-trauma-to-future-of-e-street-106550/.

21. Bob Love, "Bruce Springsteen: The Boss Talks about Family, Creativity, Love and Loss in Our Exclusive In-Depth Interview," *AARP: The Magazine,* October/November 2020. https://press.aarp.org/2020-24-9-Bruce-Springsteen -Talks-New-Album-AARP-The-Magazine.

22. Bob Love, "Helen Mirren: In Light and Shadow," *AARP: The Magazine,* December 2016/January 2017. https://www.aarp.org/entertainment/movies -for-grownups/info-2016/helen-mirren-celebrity-interview.html.

23. Leonard Cohen and Sharon Robinson, "A Thousand Kisses Deep," 2006, lyrics © Sony/ATV Music Publishing LLC.

24. Ronnie Landfield, interview with the author, October 14, 2020.

25. Jodi Long, interview with the author.

CHAPTER SIX

1. Val Garay, interview with the author, December 6, 2020.

2. Ronnie Landfield, interview with the author, October 14, 2020.

3. Dennis Quaid, interview with the author, May 1, 2021.

4. Jodi Long, interview with the author, December 24, 2020.

5. Dennis Quaid, interview with the author, May 1, 2021.

6. Ram Dass regarding using the energy of nervousness as an inner engine: personal conversation during a meditation retreat in September 1989, in Lyon, France.

7. Jack Kornfield, *Buddha's Little Instruction Book* (New York: Bantam Books, 1994), 11.

8. Glenn Frey conversation with Bob Seger, Alison Ellwood, director, Alex Gibney, co-producer, *History of the Eagles,* documentary miniseries, 2013.

9. Dennis Quaid, interview with the author, May 1, 2021.

10. Cody Fern, interview with the author, January 15, 2021.

11. Ronnie Landfield, interview with the author, October 14, 2020.

12. Amy Ziering, interview with the author, July 3, 2021.

13. Roger E. Beaty et al., "Robust Prediction of Individual Creative Ability from Brain Functional Connectivity," *Proceedings of the National Academy of Sciences of the United States of America* 115, no. 5 (January 30, 2018): 1087–92. https://www.pnas.org/content/115/5/1087. Note that according to the study, the brain regions involved in each of the three systems in the brain used effectively by highly creative people are as follows: "the default mode network, comprised of cortical midline and posterior inferior parietal regions; the executive (or frontoparietal) control network, comprised of lateral prefrontal and anterior inferior parietal regions; and the salience network, comprised of bilateral insula and anterior cingulate cortex."

CHAPTER SEVEN

1. Ellen J. Langer, *On Becoming an Artist: Reinventing Yourself through Mindful Creativity* (New York: Ballantine Books, 2005), 102.

2. David Seltzer, interview with the author.

3. Val Garay, interview with the author, December 6, 2020.

4. Ellen J. Langer, *On Becoming an Artist: Reinventing Yourself through Mindful Creativity* (New York: Ballantine Books, 2005), 49.

5. The Beatles Bible, "George Harrison Performs on Badge," October 2, 2011. https://www.beatlesbible.com/1968/11/21/george-harrison-performs-on-badge-cream/. Also, "Eric Clapton—Badge (Live Video Version-One More Car)," YouTube, posted October 27, 2009. https://youtu.be/xSAwlhrMWkU.

6. Ronnie Landfield, interview with the author, October 14, 2020.

7. Steven Soderbergh, *Sex, Lies, and Videotape* (New York: Harper & Row, 1990), epigraph.

8. Val Garay, interview with the author, December 6, 2020.

9. Dennis Quaid, interview with the author.

10. Ibid.

11. Amy Ziering, interview with the author, July 3, 2021.

12. Dennis Quaid, interview with the author.

13. Jonathan Scales, interview with the author, November 20, 2020.

14. Glen Frey on elbow grease, time, thought, and persistence. Alison Ellwood, director, Alex Gibney, co-producer. *History of the Eagles,* documentary miniseries.

15. Alison Wood Brooks et al., "Don't Stop Believing: Rituals Improve Performance by Decreasing Anxiety," *Organizational Behavior and Human Decision Processes* 137 (2016): 71–85. https://www.hbs.edu/ris/Publication%20Files/Rituals%20OBHDP_5cbc5848-ef4d-4192-a320-68d30169763c.pdf.

16. Amy Ziering, interview with the author, July 3, 2021.

17. Personal conversation with Tom Hayden, circa May 1987 at the home of Katie and David Phillips during a Tom Hayden fundraiser.

18. Mason Currey, *Daily Rituals: How Artists Work* (New York: Alfred A. Knopf, 2013), 74.

19. Ronnie Landfield, interview with the author, October 14, 2020.

20. David Seltzer, interview with the author.

21. Ibid.

22. Chris Choy, phone interview with the author, April 2021.

23. Mason Currey, *Daily Rituals*, 72.

24. Jack Canfield, *The Success Principles: How to Get from Where You Are to Where You Want to Be* (New York: William Morrow, 2005, 2015).

CHAPTER EIGHT

1. Kay Jamison Redfield, *Touched with Fire: Manic Depressive Illness and the Artistic Temperament* (New York: Free Press Paperbacks, 1993).

2. Leonard Cohen on his depression and his creativity. Mikal Gilmore, "Leonard Cohen: Remembering the Life and Legacy of the Poet of Brokenness," *Rolling Stone,* November 30, 2016. https://www.rollingstone.com/music/music-features/leonard-cohen-remembering-the-life-and-legacy-of-the-poet-of-brokenness-192994/.

3. Bruce Springsteen on balancing friction and tension in his songwriting. Brian Hiatt, "True Bruce: Springsteen Goes Deep, from Early Trauma to the Future of E Street: Rocker Opens Up about His Life, Expanding on Revelations in Candid New Memoir 'Born to Run,'" *Rolling Stone,* October 5, 2016. https://www.rollingstone.com/music/music-features/true-bruce-springsteen-goes-deep-from-early-trauma-to-future-of-e-street-106550/.

4. Springsteen on talk therapy. Bob Love, "Bruce Springsteen: The Boss Talks about Family, Creativity, Love and Loss in Our Exclusive In-Depth Interview," *AARP: The Magazine* (October/November 2020). https://press.aarp.org/2020-24-9-Bruce-Springsteen-Talks-New-Album-AARP-The-Magazine.

5. David Seltzer, interview with the author.

6. Ruth Ann Atchley et al., "Creativity in the Wild: Improving Creative Reasoning through Immersion in Natural Settings," *PLoS ONE* 7, no. 12 (2012): e51474. doi: 10.1371/journal.pone.0051474.

7. You can learn more about intergenerational trauma at the American Psychological Association's website by reading the article "The Legacy of Trauma" by Tori DeAngelis, *Monitor on Psychology* 50, no. 2 (February 2019). https://www.apa.org/monitor/2019/02/legacy-trauma.

8. Editorial Staff of the American Addiction Centers, "Ibogaine Success Rate and Treatment Centers Near Me," AmericanAddictionCenters.org, June 16, 2021 (updated November 3, 2021). https://americanaddictioncenters.org/meth-treatment/success-rate-for-ibogaine, retrieved June 27, 2021.

9. Andrew Jacobs, "The Psychedelic Revolution Is Coming. Psychiatry May Never Be the Same," *New York Times,* May 10, 2021. https://www.nytimes.com/2021/05/09/health/psychedelics-mdma-psilocybin-molly-mental-health.html?searchResultPosition=1.

10. "Ram Dass Gives Maharaji The 'Yogi Medicine,'" https://www.ramdass.org/ram-dass-gives-maharaji-the-yogi-medicine/. Ram Dass also told me this story in personal conversations I had with him on several occasions in Amherst, Massachusetts, and Maui, Hawaii.

11. Gretchen Reynolds, "Can Exercise Make You More Creative?" *New York Times*, Phys. Ed. section, February 3, 2021, updated February 5, 2021. https://www.nytimes.com/2021/02/03/well/exercise-creativity.html.

12. Scott Douglas, *Running Is My Therapy: Relieve Stress and Anxiety, Fight Depression, and Live Happier* (New York: The Experiment, LLC, 2018).

13. Bessel A. van der Kolk et al., "Yoga as an Adjunctive Treatment for Posttraumatic Stress Disorder: A Randomized Controlled Trial," *Journal of Clinical Psychiatry* 75, no. 6 (June 2014): e559–65. https://pubmed.ncbi.nlm.nih.gov/25004196/.

14. Ronald A. Alexander and Elisha Goldstein, "Mindfulness, Trauma, and Trance: A Mindfulness-Based Psychotherapeutic Approach," in *The Wiley Blackwell Handbook of Mindfulness and Psychotherapy,* vol. 2 (Malden, MA: John Wiley & Sons, 2014).

15. Bill W.'s 1961 letter to Carl Jung. Ian McCabe, *Carl Jung and Alcoholics Anonymous: The Twelve Steps as a Spiritual Journey of Individuation* (New York and London: Routledge, Taylor and Francis Group, 2018), 7. First published 2015 by Karnac Books Ltd.

16. Margarita Luttichau 1947 letter relating that Jung gave instructions on how a group model might work. Ian McCabe, *Carl Jung and Alcoholics Anonymous: The Twelve Steps as a Spiritual Journey of Individuation* (New York and London: Routledge Taylor and Francis Group, 2018), 3–4. (First published 2015 by Karnac Books Ltd.)

17. "Stevie Nicks of Fleetwood Mac on Her Pill Addiction," *Newsweek,* May 1, 2011. https://www.newsweek.com/stevie-nicks-fleetwood-mac-her-pill -addiction-67619.

CHAPTER NINE

1. Personal conversation with Dr Milton Erickson at his home in Phoenix, Arizona, August 1975.

2. Jerren Wittenstein, "Snap Hits $100-Billion Market Value after Doubling in Four Months," *Los Angeles Times,* February 2, 2021. https://www.latimes .com/business/story/2021-02-22/snap-hits-100-billion-market-value.

3. THR staff, "5 Legendary Feuds between Artists and Record Labels," *The Hollywood Reporter,* February 8, 2018. https://www.hollywoodreporter.com /news/general-news/prince-neil-young-george-michael-417607/.

4. Albert Einstein, *Cosmic Religion: With Other Opinions and Aphorisms* (New York: Covici-Friede, 1931, republished New York: Dover Publications, 2009), 97.

Core Creativity Resources

MEDITATION AND PERSONAL GROWTH CENTERS

1440 Multiversity
Scotts Valley, California
www.1440.org

Alternatives
London, England
www.alternatives.org.uk

Esalen Institute
Big Sur, California
www.esalen.org

Hollyhock Growth Center
Cortes Island, British Columbia, Canada
https://hollyhock.ca/

Kripalu Center for Yoga and Health
Lennox, Massachusetts
www.kripalu.org

New York Open Center
New York, New York
www.opencenter.org

Omega Institute for Holistic Studies
Rhinebeck, New York
www.eomega.org

Shambhala Mountain Center
Red Feathers Lake, Colorado
www.shambhalamountain.org

The Four Winds Society
School of Energy Medicine
www.thefourwinds.com

UCLA Mindfulness Research Center
Los Angeles, California
www.marc.ucla.edu

MEDITATION AND ZEN BUDDHIST CENTERS

Barre Center for Buddhist Studies
Barre, Massachusetts
www.buddhistinquiry.org

Dzogchen Center
Training in Tibetan Buddhism with Lama Surya Das
https://dzogchen.org

Insight LA Meditation–Trudy Goodman Kornfield, PhD
Santa Monica, California
https://insightla.org

Insight Meditation Community of Washington
John Cabin, MD, and Tara Brach, PhD
www.imcw.org

Insight Meditation Society
Barre, Massachusetts
www.dharma.org

Mt. Baldy Zen Center
Rinzai Zen in Southern California
San Gabriel Mountains, California
www.mbzc.org

Mindfulness Institute—Loch Kelly
Woodstock, New York
www.effortlessmindfulness.org

Pointing Out the Great Way with Dr. Daniel P. Brown
A Unique Approach to Indo-Tibetan Spiritual Development
https://pointingoutthegreatway.com

Radiance Sutras School of Meditation
Los Angeles, California
http://www.meditationtt.com/online-meditation-teacher-training-200
-hours-certification-program-full-details

Red Feathers Lake, Colorado
www.shambhalamountain.org

San Francisco Zen Center
San Francisco, California
www.sfzc.org

Spirit Rock Meditation Center—Jack Kornfield, PhD
Woodacre, California
www.spiritrock.org

Tassajara Zen Mountain Center
Carmel Valley, California
www.sfzc.org/practice-centers/tassajara

The Center for Mindful Living
Los Angeles, California
www.mindfullivingla.org

UCLA Mindfulness Awareness Research Center
Los Angeles, California
www.marc.ucla.edu

Upaya Zen Center—Roshi Joan Halifax, PhD
Santa Fe, New Mexico
www.upaya.org

Yokoji-Zen Mountain Center
San Jacinto Mountains, California
https://zmc.org

Zen Center
Athens, Greece
www.zencenterathens.com

Zen Center of Los Angeles
Los Angeles, California
https://zcla.org

Zen Rocks Retreat Center
Peloponnese of Southern Greece
https://zenrocksmani.com

YOGA AND MEDITATION TRAININGS

Mindfulness, Yoga, and Entrepreneurship Training
Katie Brauer
www.katiebrauer.com

Prana Vinyasa Yoga with Shiva Rea, MA
Live and Online Retreats and Immersions
Samudra Global School of Living Yoga
www.pranaflow.love

Revolution Within with Seane Corn
Yoga Online Classes and Support
https://seanecorn.com

Rising Yoga Lotus
Daniel Stewart, MA
www.risinglotusyoga.com

Samata Yoga International
Yoga Therapy Training—Larry Payne, PhD
https://samata.com

Soma Psyche Sangha with Micheline Berry
Yoga Teacher Training and Immersions
www.michelineberry.com

Yoga Alliance
Center for Yoga Psychology with Ashley Turner, MA
Venice Beach, California,
www.yogaalliance.org/SchoolPublicProfile?sid=7824

PROFESSIONAL BUSINESS AND PSYCHOTHERAPY TRAINING CENTERS

A Couple of Individuals
Couples Therapy Trainings
https://acoupleofindividuals.com

Bessel van der Kolk, MD
Trauma Healing Courses
www.besselvanderkolk.com

Ergos Institute of Somatic Education
Peter A. Levine, PhD
www.somaticexperiencing.com/ergos

Guerette Symposia Series
Continuing Education Program for Mental Health Professionals
Boston, Massachusetts
https://cme.bu.edu/guerette

Institute for Meditation and Psychotherapy
https://meditationandpsychotherapy.org

Lifespan Learning Institute
Continuing Education for Mental Health Professionals
Los Angeles, California
www.lifespanlearn.org

Milton Erickson Foundation—Jeff Zeig, PhD
Phoenix, Arizona
www.erickson-foundation.org

Mindfulness Based Stress Reduction Training
Jon Kabat-Zinn
Naropa University
Boulder, Colorado
www.naropa.edu

Mindsight Institute
Daniel Siegel, MD
Online Training and In-Person Workshops
www.mindsightinstitute.com

OpenMind Training Program—Ronald Alexander, PhD
Core Creativity and Mindfulness Training for Business and Mental
Health Professionals
Santa Monica, California
www.openmindtraining.com

Psychotherapy Networker Symposium
Virtual Training and Conferences
https://www.psychnetworker.org/2021

Robert and Rita Resnick, PhD
Gestalt Associates Training Los Angeles (GATLA)
European Residential
http://gatla.org

Somatic Experiencing International
Boulder, Colorado
https://traumahealing.org

Stephen Gilligan, PhD
Self-Relations and Creative Mind
Encinitas, California
www.stephengilligan.com

The Institute for Transformational Thinking
Thought Coach Training
www.theiftt.org

INSTITUTES, ORGANIZATIONS, AND INDIVIDUALS OFFERING CREATIVITY, SUCCESS, AND LEADERSHIP TRAININGS

Jack Canfield
Coaching, Master Success, and Train the Trainer
www.jackcanfield.com

Judith Orloff, MD
Empath Support Community
www.DrJudithOrloff.com

Ruth Buczynski, PhD
Training in Mindfulness and Trauma Healing
www.nicabm.com/faculty/ruth-buczynski/

Tony Robbins
Trainings in Human Potential
www.tonyrobbins.com

ORGANIZATIONS OFFERING SUPPORT
FOR PEOPLE WITH BIPOLAR DISORDER

Bipolar and Depression Outcomes Research Institute
www.bdori.org

Bipolar Advantage
https://www.bipolaradvantage.com
Tom Wootton

Bibliography

Alexander, Ronald. *Wise Mind, Open Mind: Finding Purpose and Meaning in Times of Crisis, Loss, and Change*. Oakland, CA: New Harbinger Publications, 2008.

Alexander, Ronald A., and Goldstein, Elisha. "Mindfulness, Trauma, and Trance: A Mindfulness-Based Psychotherapeutic Approach." In *The Wiley Blackwell Handbook of Mindfulness and Psychotherapy*, vol. 2. Malden, MA: John Wiley & Sons, 2014.

Benson, Herbert, with Miriam Z. Klipper. *The Relaxation Response*. New York: William Morrow and Company, Inc., 1975.

Bonny, Helen L., and Louis M. Savary, *Music and Your Mind: Listening with a New Consciousness*. Barrytown, NY: Station Press, 1990.

Canfield, Jack, and Switzer, Janet. *The Success Principles™: How to Get from Where You Are to Where You Want to Be*. New York: William Morrow, 2005.

Csikszentmihalyi, Mihaly. *Flow: The Psychology of Optimal Experience*. New York: HarperCollins Publishers, 1990.

Currey, Mason. *Daily Rituals: How Artists Work*. New York: Alfred A. Knopf, 2013.

Douglas, Scott. *Running Is My Therapy: Relieve Stress and Anxiety, Fight Depression, and Live Happier*. New York: The Experiment, LLC, 2018.

Einstein, Albert. *Cosmic Religion: With Other Opinions and Aphorisms*. New York: Covici-Friede, 1931, republished New York: Dover Publications, 2009.

Emerick, Geoff, with Massey, Howard. *Here, There and Everywhere: My Life Recording the Music of The Beatles*. New York: Gotham Books, 2006.

Epstein, Mark. "Awakening with Prozac." *Tricyle* (Fall), 1993. https://tricycle
.org/magazine/awakening-prozac/.

Everett, Walter. *The Beatles as Musicians: Revolver through the Anthology.*
New York: Oxford University Press, 1999.

Fadiman, James. *The Psychedelic Explorer's Guide: Safe, Therapeutic, and
Sacred Journeys.* Rochester, VT: Inner Traditions, 2011.

Gilbert, Elizabeth. *Big Magic: Creative Living beyond Fear.* New York: Penguin Random House, 2015.

Hayden, Tom. *Reunion: A Memoir,* New York: Crowell-Collier Publishing
Company, 1989.

James, William. *The Varieties of Religious Experience.* Originally published by
Longmans, Green and Co. 1902. New York: Random House, The Modern
Library, 1929.

Kornfield, Jack. *Buddha's Little Instruction Book.* New York: Bantam Books,
1994.

Langer, Ellen J. *On Becoming an Artist: Reinventing Yourself through Mindful
Creativity.* New York: Ballantine Books, 2005.

Levine, Peter A. *Waking the Tiger: Healing Trauma.* Berkeley, CA: North
Atlantic Books, 1997.

Martin, George, with Pearson, William. *With a Little Help from My Friends:
The Making of Sgt. Pepper.* Boston: Little Brown & Co, 1995.

McCabe, Ian. *Carl Jung and Alcoholics Anonymous: The Twelve Steps as a
Spiritual Journey of Individuation.* New York and London: Routledge, Taylor and Francis Group, 2018. (First published 2015 by Karnac Books Ltd.)

Orloff, Judith. *Guide to Intuitive Healing: 5 Steps to Physical, Emotional and
Sexual Wellness.* New York: Harmony Books, 2001.

Ray, Amit. *Meditation: Insights and Inspiration.* n.p.: Inner Light Publishers,
2015.

Redfield, Kay Jamison. *Touched by Fire: Manic Depressive Illness and the
Artistic Temperament.* New York: Free Press Paperbacks, 1993.

Soderbergh, Steven. *Sex, Lies, and Videotape Movie Edition Screenplay.* New
York: Harper & Row, 1990.

Van der Kolk, Bessel A. *The Body Keeps the Score: Brain, Mind and Body in
the Healing of Trauma.* New York: Penguin Books, 2014.

Index

consciousness, 20–21, 34; beta, 14; self-consciousness, 23; studies, 129; waking, 69, 83. *See also* open mind consciousness
constructive criticism, 67–68
Consulting a Mentor visualization, 53–54, 172, 181
contentment, 26
conversations, 22; imaginary, 54; in-person, 59
Conversations with Artists (Rodman), 47
cortisol, 19, 24, 29, 82
Cosmic Religion (Einstein), 159
countertransference, 50
COVID-19 pandemic, 2, 115
crash, car, 154–55
creativity: discipline for, 1, 2; embracing, 3–5; as key skill, 3; in late life, 5; reclaiming, 31–35. *See also specific topics*
Creativity Support Pod, 10, 45–46, 60–61, 68, 160, 172–73; accountability provided by, 57, 58, 89; facilitator for, 59
credit, giving yourself, 175, 176, 183
Crichton, Michael, 92
criticism, 60, 61, 67–68. *See also* inner critic
crying, 38, 154
Csikszentmihalyi, Mihaly, 6, 188n10
curiosity, 11, 68, 74, 75, 98, 111–12
Currey, Mason, 124
cynicism, 8, 23, 96, 97

Daily Rituals (Currey), 124
danger, 3, 19, 78–81, 136, 140
data management, digital, 48, 49
Day in the Future visualization, 34–35, 102, 173, 182
deadlines, 148
debt, 104

decision-making, 165; analytical, 159–61; false beliefs about, 160; fear and, 148–51; intuitive, 96, 147, 152–53, 159–61; journaling for, 157–58; moving into, 156–59; past, 157–59; timing, 163–64; tuning in within for, 151–53
default mode network, 95, 193n13
defensiveness, 5, 53, 68
Department of Imagineering, Disney, 25–26
depression, 130–31, 135
Dick, Kirby, 62, 63
diet, 118, 119, 133, 134, 141
digital data management, 48, 49
directors, 59–60
disappointment, 110
disease, 118, 119
Disney, 25–26
dissatisfaction, 64
"distractive fat," 104
divergent thinking, 7, 16
diversity, in Wisdom Council of Support, 54–57
Douglas, Scott, 141
dreams, 77–80, 85, 155–56; breakthroughs from, 24; lucid, 81–82; recurring, 81; as tools, 71, 82
Dychtwald, Ken, 123
Dylan, Bob, 92–93

ego, 28, 56, 60, 87, 88, 96–97
Einstein, Albert, 10, 159
Elaine (client), 153–55
Eli Lilly company, 128
emotions, 6, 12, 13, 26; art and, 37–38; harnessing, 36; meditation and, 14–15; mindfulness shifting, 20–22; releasing, 39
encouragement, 10, 11
entertainment attorneys, 107–5

About the Author

Ronald A. Alexander, PhD, is a psychotherapist who is a mindfulness trainer, a creativity, business, and leadership coach, and an international trainer of healthcare professionals, lay people, and businesses. He also has a private psychotherapy and executive coaching practice in Santa Monica, California. He is the executive director of the OpenMind® Training Program, a leading-edge organization that offers personal and professional training programs in mindfulness-based mind-body therapies, transformational leadership, and meditation. He is the author of the highly acclaimed book *Wise Mind, Open Mind: Finding Purpose and Meaning in Times of Crisis, Loss, and Change* (2008) and two meditation CDs.

Ronald Alexander's extensive training includes Somatic Experiencing, Ericksonian Mind-Body Therapies, conflict management, gestalt therapy, leadership, and organizational development. He pioneered the early values and vision-based models for current-day leadership and professional coaching. Alexander has been teaching mind-body therapies, mindfulness meditation, creative visualization, and transpersonal psychology since 1970 throughout the United States, Canada, the United Kingdom, Europe, Russia, Asia, Japan, and Australia. His specialty is combining Eastern and Western techniques that support strategies of personal and corporate excellence, including creativity, leadership and communication skills, and conflict resolution.

Alexander's consulting and coaching clients include artistic talent, management, and production staff in the motion picture, television, and music industries, such as Universal Pictures, Sony Entertainment (film and music), Walt Disney Studios, ABC Television, Telemundo, RCA, MCA, and DGC. He has also provided leadership and coaching training for employees from computer and software companies, including Apple Computer, Microsoft, and Sun Microsystems.

DrRon@RonaldAlexander.com
www.CoreCreativity.com
www.RonaldAlexander.com

CPSIA information can be obtained
at www.ICGtesting.com
Printed in the USA
BVHW031405020422
633068BV00002B/2